THE
APOCALYPSE

THE
APOCALYPSE

Historical Fiction on the Third Reich

EDWARD DELIA

VIZE PUBLICATIONS
NEW YORK

The Apocalypse
Copyright © 2004 by Edward DeLia

International Standard Book Number: 1-929612-60-5
Library of Congress Catalog Number: 2004093499

PRINTED IN THE UNITED STATES OF AMERICA

VIZE PUBLISHING COMPANY
PO BOX 402
NESCONSET, NEW YORK 11767

ADAMS PRESS
CHICAGO, ILLINOIS

To My Mother

Death comes to all life which does not
fulfill the divine meaning and the divine truth.

–Nikolai Berdyaev, *The Destiny of Man*

TABLE OF CONTENTS

AUTHOR'S NOTE

The following is a work of historical fiction and philosophy. As historical fiction, it is a mixture of creation and historical fact. All historical sources are scrupulously cited; all persons or institutions not so cited are entirely fictional—above all, Bertrand Sovare. His life and memories are a mirror to an age of chaos.

This story is the record of a vision. It is not meant to be a philosophy of life or a prescription for ethics. And it does not embody my personal autobiography. It is a record of the main protagonist—a bitter man and former Nazi—and his horrific insights into his experience and the nature of the Third Reich.

EDWARD DELIA
MAY 12, 2003

CHAPTER ONE

What I record here is a memoir to myself. A record of my life, my experience, my world. That world is mine—it is me—and is peculiar only to me. It is not yours—it is not you—and it is not for you. It is merely a record of events as I recall them now, no doubt colored by my specific makeup and character; yet, despite the imperfections of my memory, not to mention the physical decline of my person, I have little doubt that what now ensues corresponds to what actually happened during my captivity. Only I can be sure of that, but once again these pages are meant only for my perusal.

Nonetheless, should the end come suddenly and the flames not consume this tract, foreign eyes might violate my chambers to be apprized of the inmost secrets of my soul. (My soul! Ha, it's incredible how in a turn of speech you refer to what your deepest convictions deny, or perhaps those convictions are betrayed by the feelings ingrained therein.) In any case, keep in mind that I mention you only in light of this contingency—nay, this risk—which in a gambling spirit I accept in order to make my past more real to myself. For these words rekindle yesterday and allow me to recapture what is no more as if it were here now—to salvage from the dregs of a wasted life some meaning. And meaning, after all, both in its attainment and denial rouses men to absurd action and endless strife. It drives a cripple to conjure up the scene of that dreadful accident; it moves a beggar to walk unnoticed through the streets of his former neighborhood; it alone is the source of this reminiscence.

I belabor all this so you will avoid the misunderstanding that I enter these notes for you. You must not think that I care about your welfare or hope your future will elude the fabric of my past. To the contrary, I prefer just the opposite. If my experiences were malignant, why should yours be benign? Your dreams are no more dear! And neither is the quality of your humanity more pure nor the excretions from your bowels less base! Indeed, I have no desire to enhance your safety or future merriment. To be honest, for every sorrow in my life, I wish the same, if not worse, for you.

But, you will say, this is perverse for the very purpose of recording the past is to improve ourselves: to learn from our mistakes so they will not be repeated. *Our* mistakes! You have the arrogance to connect yourself with me simply because we both are human; simply because we both have two arms and legs and hands and feet; simply because both of us walk on the same earth and glance at the same sky. From this you say *our* mistakes? As if I could care for you or you for me; as if my experience and yours had any common term; as if my existence were essential to yours or yours to mine. Nay! There is no humanity between us, no common concern, and you show this beneath your veneer of bourgeois morality—for you prize yourself above me. Indeed, you value my life so cheaply as to regard it only as a crucible, a mere experiment, for insight conductive to your blissful destiny. Did you ever consider that your cheerful future would not undo my tragedy? The beauty of your utopia is not just payment for the flesh and blood agony which is mine alone, for my pain endures. It endures as a primary datum of evil, a hole in the fabric of all optimism. Even if evil should be banished from the earth for all time, even if man should ultimately become perfect, even if Christ should return to establish his eternal kingdom, it would remain as an indelible stain of imperfection. This agony, this lonely pain, would still cry to the heavens for explanation.

CHAPTER TWO

The period of my life, which I now call the Apocalypse because it symbolized the end of my world, probably began in mid-September during the third year of the war. I remember awakening from a swoon one fine summer evening with the letter that was to be the instrument of my destruction still crushed in my hand, a telegram instructing me to report to the Munich Y Depot for reeducation—a euphemism for relocation in those days. It was conveyed to me the previous day at the university, its first melancholy words leaving a deep impression. It began: "You are hereby instructed to report...." Instructed! I pondered for a moment. An unwelcome message, no doubt. But, also, an incomprehensible one. Such notes were common in those days, but only in the case of subversive individuals or convicted criminals. Was I to be ranked with them? I had always been a loyal party member and supported Hitler's policies with precision in private and at the university. How, then, could I receive such a lamentable telegram? I thought about it continuously. Yet, I could think of no possible infraction of party rules that might have incriminated me.

Perhaps there had been a mistake. Yes, an error. Errors do occur, you know. (Ha, I thought of Schopenhauer's remark that human life itself was some sort of mistake.) So what could be more convenient than to assume that this turn of events had originated in one. My university colleagues thought so. They offered sympathy—mostly insincere. But, their sympathy did not translate into practical advice on how to relieve the situation. You know, there is nothing more useless than casual acquaintances. Mere role players! They smile and smile and mean nothing by these smiles. Earlstein and Benitz, in particular—two useless nonentities. Pushing them aside, I made several subsequent inquiries at the Ministries of the Interior and later at the Posts but received few relevant details. Yet, the message's veracity was unquestioned. So while I was given no specific reason for this instruction, I reported to the railroad depot on the appointed day.

At the depot a sense of anomie overtook me. The world around me seemed so alien and detached, as if it were the product of some inhuman despot. A hideous feeling that was exacerbated upon seeing the several uniformed guards around me. I approached one, a bald, stocky, expressionless young man, quite gross in his features.

"Your papers," he said curtly.

I handed him the telegram. He then looked down at his log, making entries with a certain annoyance.

"Jew," he grunted.

I replied loudly. "I am not a Jew."

"Jew," he said again.

"No," I retorted, "I'm not Jewish. I've been given no reason for this action. I insist on an explanation."

He glanced back at me with anger. "What you must do now is board Locomotive Number 12."

I protested vehemently. "Where am I going?"

"All information will be given to you upon arrival," he repeated with increasing agitation.

Again I protested, "Am I not entitled...?"

"All information will be given to you upon arrival," he screamed as if a universal truth was embodied in the phrase. (Or perhaps that truth was the shield it provided against thinking about or confronting any moral situation.)

Once again, "What you must do now is leave your petty belongings and board." He then pointed to an adjacent area. Quite shaken, I feigned a calmness that I did not feel and proceeded to take my place on the dreary railcar.

Upon boarding, I looked at the sky. Dark, aggressive, overhanging clouds subsisting in such disharmony with the green, rustic exterior below. I glanced at them with almost a sense of the sublime; how I could conceive of such things then is now beyond me. Nonetheless, I did gaze. Somehow, only momentarily, I thought of the difference between the outer beauty of the world and the ugliness of sin; of the contrast between the majesty of creation and the moral baseness of mankind. Yet, the two are often indistinguishable, and the majestic is sometimes morally base—which reminds me of the first time I saw Hitler. It was like looking at a god—a paragon. It was September 1934. He walked magnificently between two long, extended columns of humanity. His uniform and bright red garb were brilliant. To look at him was to see history being shaped by the will of one man. It produced an exalted, noble feeling, one bred of deep, inner satisfaction. From this beginning, how, oh how, did the situation sour to this barren state of affairs?

Suddenly, other people began to board. Then there were many others. One grabbed me; another shoved me. Gradually, I was elbowed to the side of the car by the animal force of those around me. Criminals! Subhumans, no doubt, worthy only of destruction. I kept thinking: what was I doing here with them? I then heard a loud, shrieking noise followed by a discernible pounding. The massive door was closing. The SS Guards stood erect outside preventing anyone from fleeing amidst the wailings and lamentations. One women cried, "Don't shut the door!"

Another said, "There's no air. Let us out." Mothers fainted, children screamed, men groaned. There were no openings through which to see the sunlight except for the tiny cracks between the ceiling boards. Yet, even this dribble of light was appreciated. In what seemed to be an endless interval, we rode like this, closely packed and in misery, until long after embarkation. I tried not to think of the people around me. Slaves and subhumans! I hated them. Were they not Germany's ruination and the cause of all our misery? Devils! The authors of the "stab in the back"! I turned away in disgust and glanced at the wall. I thought of nothing in particular, a nothingness that almost empties one of anxiety. The heat then soared again, and the stench of human sweat became unbearable. I leaned against the side of the car, my eyes fixed on the myriads of tiny dots within each board that seemingly comprised their own infinity. In this semiconscious state, I rested and waited for some relief. None came quickly. It was just an endless ride, seemingly to nowhere.

CHAPTER THREE

Then after what seemed to be hours or perhaps days, the locomotive finally slowed down, coming to a shrieking, loud, yet firm halt. I waited in anticipation for the mammoth gray door to open as my fingers caressed its thick grooves and crevices. And after a time it did. As I left, after elbowing and shoving several people, the coolness of the air immediately refreshed me. The guards directed us to walk up a long entrance way where a low level, yet quite extensive building with a side unloading area, slowly came into view. The foliage was green, fresh, and well preserved. A large sign read "R.K. Titnan." I felt a finger on my shoulder: "What do they make here?"

"I don't know," I answered with some irritation.

We were led through a corridor and seated in an enormous room with a gray-white interior. I glanced around the room while a SS Guard mounted the podium. He spoke: "My name is Berger. I am in command. My task is to ensure compliance. You are here because you are criminals. Some of your crimes are great, others' lesser. But all of you must work off your debt to the Reich. If you don't, you will be executed. Here at Titnan we produce relays that are vital to the war effort. Now, each of you will be called in turn and assigned your duties."

He then slowly jumped off the platform and walked into a small room adjacent to the stage area. There were over a hundred men in the larger room and I waited my turn. My mind wandered to and fro as I tried to

7

grasp the meaning of the events that had brought me to this fate. Then Berger announced in a loud, firm voice: " Bertrand Sovare." Shaking slightly, I immediately walked into the side room. I thought it was strange that Berger himself would be meeting me. But, he was. The SS Commander looked up, greeted me curtly, and proceeded to describe my assignment. I would be taught to operate a punch press and various screw machines. I, however, was more interested in expressing my discontent about my alleged misdemeanors. I inquired. Berger then looked down at a folder and said harshly, "You are being detained for political crimes."

I retorted cynically, "What are they?"

"Simply this: teaching subversive materials and quoting from books that have been banned," he bluntly replied.

I answered, "What teachings?"

"For one, Marx. You have continuously quoted his social doctrines," he said.

I interrupted. "You cannot be serious!"

"Mr. Sovare," he replied as he raised his right hand, "I have many others to see. You have your assignment. Now, you must take your place."

"But...," I began to protest ineffectively.

"Please," he sneered, "maybe one day you will discuss the matter in front of the People's Court. For now, you must take your place." The audience was over!

I was immediately escorted into the factory and was surrounded by machines—huge oak machines—producing complex mechanical parts. After being shown a few basic procedures, I began work.

On the first day, I labored for sixteen hours. On the second, the same. By the end of the week, it would be obvious that, with little variation, this would be my routine. Hard work. Few breaks. Poor food. No conversation; it was prohibited. Occasionally, some of my fellow sufferers would try to initiate conversation. I gave them no encouragement—even in the case of one pretty woman. I only looked at her. I feared detection by the SS and by now thoroughly detested people. At the end of each day, I was led to a corridor and told to sleep on the floor. Always, the same pattern followed day after day.

As I performed my functions routinely and without complaint, my mind served as the only outlet to freedom since all else was completely regulated. Indeed, my mind became a panorama of the past—my past— a past plagued by probing questions and horrible memories. I kept asking myself one question: what was I, Bertrand Sovare, doing here? What horrible sequence of events—indeed, what malignancy in nature—could have led me to this fate? Bertrand Sovare: scholar, family man, teacher, and author of the most profound work on Kant. How did I fall to this state?

Although I did not know it then, the short-term answer was that this was all part of a slave empire being set up by the SS throughout Europe. Millions of foreigners and occasionally some domestic nationals were being engaged in slave labor. Some were prisoners of war; others were unfortunate people simply torn away from their communities by force. All were reduced to the status of slaves as in Rome under Caesar Augustus. I was one of them. We worked to maintain war production that was being seriously curtailed by the Anglo-American air attacks. We had no rights. In Hitler's mind, we had no right to live unless we toiled for Germany.

Never before had the problem of evil pressed so heavily upon me. And the problem was personal, not a series of abstractions. It concerned flesh and blood, not merely ideas. It was more than a typical textbook syllogism. It affected the pulp that was mine alone. How could an all- good, all-powerful God tolerate the multitudes of evil surrounding me? How could Christ tolerate the suffering, the mischief, the impiety? God—nah, let's face it—there is no God! Years ago, I plagued myself with the question of how I could know for sure. Now I do. Ask me for proof of God's nonexistence, and I answer: Bertrand Sovare is in this state! Bertrand Sovare is living in drudgery, toil and disgrace! If there was a God, this would not be!

Now, when I say there is no God, I mean *there is no principle of benevolence in relation to me.* I mean there is no abstract purpose, no moral concern or no star to guide my destiny. I mean chaos abounds, chance is prime, good seldom wins, and evil is often triumphant. Above all, I mean whatever happens, happens! The noblest good and the most cataclysmic evil can occur under the sun. (And never was a meeting of two atoms hampered by moral concerns.) The bullet that severs my spine obeys the same laws as a benign projectile, and no moral agent will intervene to intercept its path.

I kept thinking: could man, that depraved creature, really have descended from above, from the finger of God? Or rather, from the depths of the jungle, from below, as he deserves and to which he will again devolve? The record of the foulness of his heart, the wretchedness of his aims, the wickedness of his deeds could fill the pages of a thousand volumes. What else but injustice, jealousy, hatred, strife, and war have been his legacy? Man has done more than perfect the way of Cain. He has based his entire civilization on human carnage. When I think of the insurrections, riots and purges in the last decade alone, I must conclude that God must be all merciful, or he would crush this vile race in a second. One thing is certain: if man ever becomes extinct, he will be the first species to deserve extinction.

Yet, occasionally, a sharp noise from the plant interrupted my more philosophical endeavors, and I was forced to continue the simple mechanical tasks that had now become routine. No day was extreme at Titnan, just a prosaic monotony; a gradual decline into hell by degrees—slow degrees. Sleep lasted a few hours; the toil was endless. Also, the food was putrid and the water foul. A plate of cereal or a tablespoon of salt. Under these circumstances, it again occurred to me that my freedom here derived only from the manner in which I used my mind. My body was bound by this small space and time, but my mind was capable of thinking of the past and the future, the real or the fictitious, the exalted or the profane or the serious and the comical. (I never choose the latter!) It was the sole vehicle of my liberation.

I kept thinking of the origins of the Nazi Party and the reasons for Hitler's success. Hitler's personal qualities were the main source of his rise to power: his intellect, his will, his oratorical talents, and his organizational ability. But, these qualities would not have ensured success without certain extraneous elements that provided him with the opportunity for triumph. The foremost of these was an event that occurred when Hitler was twenty-five years old: the start of World War I. Until 1914, Hitler was a failure in almost every aspect of his life. He had no place in the conservative, aristocratic world of the old Europe. He was a vagabond and in all likelihood would have remained one. This horrible war, however, destroyed the world of the old Europe that had relegated Hitler to such ignominy. A social world that evolved over centuries was overturned in a few years, and most traditional ideas seemed obsolete in a universe dominated by headlines about Verdun and the Somme. Yet, few knew exactly how to replace them. Men need values and norms to guide them; without this man is nothing. Hitler provided a replacement: Nazism was a new culture or a new set of ideas on how to live. In a world shattered by war, this was Hitler's opportunity. He took full advantage of it.

Hitler's cultural revolution had its roots deep in German history and philosophy. Autocracy, militarism and anti-Semitism were consistent with the German past; the democracy of the Weimar Republic was not. Germany had never known democracy, but it had always been ruled by autocrats. It was absurd to believe that the German Republic could survive in a post-war Europe—a Europe in chaos and distress. The leaders of the armed forces owed the new regime no loyalty, and the general population blamed the democratic chiefs for the 1918 surrender. The Republic was doomed from the start. No social order can succeed if it is functionally incongruent with that society's past— and doom is certain if there was a great revolutionary leader at the gates. And Hitler was there.

Moreover, the Weimar Regime could not ensure the public safety. During the late twenties, there was street fighting almost every night in Berlin between the Nazis and the Communists; and the forces of the Republic were lame in preventing it. "Adolf Hitler devours Karl Marx," a popular Nazi slogan at the time, tells it all. The casualties mounted daily, and little was done. It was almost as if the democrats were afraid. They were impotent. In foreign affairs, Germany was at the mercy of hostile powers, and the army was limited to only one hundred thousand men. It is easy to understand why Hitler's demand for public order and the restoration of a great German army were so popular.

Also, the economic downturn was disastrous. In 1929, the Great Depression had spread throughout Germany, resulting in mass unemployment and the ruination of the middle class. A strong middle class is the best defense against revolution, and this class was devastated. Despair, homelessness, and suicide followed. "How many thousands," Hitler shouted at a crowd in Berlin, "will put their heads in the gas ovens today because they cannot tolerate living one more day—one more hour?" Revolution was imminent!

It would be fueled by the Republic's original sin, the unjust Treaty of Verailles, which ended the Great War. This treaty tore away provinces, such as Danzig, which were previously part of Germany; imposed huge reparations upon the German people; and placed the blame for the war entirely on Germany. The unjust nature of this treaty has been condemned by nearly all historians. Hitler adroitly put the blame on the "November Criminals," a phrase that he pounded into the minds of the people. In Munich, I, myself, recall his describing the sufferings of the nation—the bread lines, the inflation, the misery—and then raising his hands dramatically and saying: "All this is the product of the men of November 1918, all of it their doing, all of it their handiwork." Men love scapegoats—myself included. The Jews and the Communists were the November Criminals, and we wanted them crushed into a thousand pieces along with their damned Versailles Treaty.

You see, the future dictator had a quality that many other leaders, including the Communist Chief Thaelmann, lacked: courage. Here was a man with a crushing will to power, one who was willing to die for his beliefs. A man willing to die can change the world since all social control is based on a desire to preserve life. Give up that desire, and worlds will crash and crumble. Add to this that he knew what he wanted to do and had the oratorical ability to deliver the message clearly. In 1932, people felt that they were wasting their lives away and despaired for a solution. Hitler had that solution and an answer to every problem. Now, no one was sure whether he was right, but desperate men will try anything. Hitler would tell them: "I am one of you. I lived in poverty, as you. I fought in the Great War, as you. And, above all, I was ruined by the Jews, as you." No other leader in the history of Germany could claim this. This was a nation that was ruled by autocrats and kings. In Hitler; we Germans could view our petty struggles as being bound up with the destiny of one man. One man whose success was a triumph of the will.

That triumph came on January 30, 1933, when Hitler was appointed Chancellor by President Hindenburg. Hitler never had a majority, but his powerful showing in the previous year's election set the stage. His opponents undercut each other by their petty intrigues and their failure to unify against him. This is especially true of General Kurt von Schleicher and Vice- Chancellor Franz von Papen, who were engaged in a game of double dealing and intrigue. The former plotted against the later and vice versa. During one of these intrigues, von Papen suggested to Hindenburg that Hitler should be appointed. On such petty motives, history often turns.

That be as it may! In any case, it occurred to me that man is thrown into a world of two common dimensions, namely, time and space. Confined spaces were everywhere. But time, that mysterious force, seemed to disappear at Titnan. It remained for me only as a chronicle of numbers laced with woe. And the numbers read July 6, 1944. It could, however, have been any month from that period since it was always the same monotonous routine—invariably the same tale of misery. Unknown to me, there were student uprisings at the University of Munich. Students were marching for freedom and peace. I now realize that this insurrection was personally damaging since my alleged misdemeanor was committed there. It was inevitable, therefore, that the strong hand of the state would come down grievously upon me.

One day two SS men whom I had not seen before accosted me. One wore tin-rimmed glasses; the other had a nasty scar that was half concealed under his ruffled coat collar. "Sovare," the latter shouted vehemently as he raised his arm in a stern manner.

"Odd-looking fellows," I murmured in a scarcely audible tone.

"Get up, you are going to Berlin," he ordered.

"Hell," I responded with defiance.

He answered: "You will stand trial before the People's Court. The charge is sedition."

I inquired no more. I was numb! I felt so low, so weak, so insignificant. I thought constantly of my state. Will there ever be a day when I'll be happy, or is happiness itself merely a mirage? Maybe, it would have been better, as Schopenhauer suggested, if the earth, no more than the moon, could call forth the accident of life, and if here as there, the surface was still in an unaffected form. So I thought! Later, I was flown to Berlin.

CHAPTER FOUR

A fter the flight, which was horrible, I was incarcerated at a detention center adjacent to the People's Court. Interred in a narrow
cell and given scant rations, I did little for days. A tactile sense of
imagery and a vague sense of the past combined to form a steady flux of
ideas. My mind wandered to and fro—from thought to thought and from
image to image. I thought mainly of the men who were responsible for my
plight. Men! Those monsters! Indeed, demons! At times, I even wonder
why man constitutes a species. Maybe the "the sick species," to take a
phrase from Nietzsche, or the breakable animal. No doubt, the animal
that plunders. What do men have in common anyway? Besides, that is, a
capacity to maraud, manipulate and to murder? His common nature is
only anatomical; his spirit remains diffuse, indeed, bifurcated. Christ
cried: "Come out of the man, thou unclean spirit." And the spirit
answered: "My name is Legion; for we are many." In this way, all men are
Legion! Legions of malice! Multiplicities of self-indulgence. Evil spirits
devouring others with glee.

But, note! The greatest of all devourers, Adolf Hitler, was merely a natural product of European society. He did not descend from the sky, but
from the womb of our bifurcated race. In this sense, he is almost a logical
deduction from the concept of man. (And this is, no doubt, what Hess
meant when he called him pure reason incarnate.) Yes, I like the beauty of
this syllogism. Given a species of a common nature, it is certain that one

should emerge who exhibits that nature to an extreme degree. Ergo: given premises A and B, then C. How logical and sequential! But, here our abstractions have wretched consequences. A tragic tautology at best, I must say. A bestial race produced a beast. A race of angels surely would not. Hitler, after all, only reflected the excesses in human nature. His extremes were the harvest of the "little evil" in all of us.

Ah, yes. And don't demean the importance of little evil: the petty hatreds or trivial resentments, the puny struggles and minute injustices, the mild vanities or unpretentious jealousies or the countless slights and brief antagonisms that constitute so much of daily life. Are not these little evils responsible for the monstrosity we call the world? Is this not a pygmy that yields a behemoth? Yes, little evil embodied in nameless, faceless people is now and has always been the anchor of tyranny. We are, of course, more comfortable with magnified wickedness and monstrous injustice. We gain solace when there is a great distance between ourselves and those we abhor. We relish the clear boundary and delight in the pretense that some moral malignancy is "out there" rather than precisely in our chests. Yet, has not the moral malignancy in us all fashioned all this? More than one-third of the people supported Hitler in 1932. And without this support he could never have become Chancellor the next year. We are responsible for this leviathan of hate.

Let us consider Hitler's father, Alois. He was an abusive, violent parent. Adolf hated him—and for good reason. And we all should hate him. The beatings Adolf received were returned upon others many times over in the years that followed. Brutality breeds brutality. Consider Hitler's mother, Klara. An overindulgent parent whom Adolf deeply loved. She was struck down by cancer at an early age. Cancer! What a horrible disease! It can reduce one to nothing. Yet, it did enrich her Jewish doctor. I hate doctors. Callous, evil beings who love controlling your destiny. I wish that I could shoot every one of them. No doubt, the young Adolf hated them, too. Also, consider Hitler's friends and reference groups: anti-Semitic peers, extremist military gangs or ultra-nationalist philosophers. Some examples would be Houston Stewart Chamberlain, Ernst Roehm, or Dietrich Eckart. The former was a racist, and the latter was a drunken writer. Roehm was a savage murderer. No wonder Hitler's ideas were deviant—deviant ideas stem from warped influences. As for his close friends, Hitler had none except, perhaps, Albert Speer, who was his personal architect. In his youth, he had August Kubizek, but he later lost contact with him.

Hitler would often describe his grandiose dreams of a future Reich with the young August, whom he met again years later in the new Nazi Austria. It was a friendly exchange—unusual for Hitler, who usually killed his former associates. I guess there are contradictions even in a tyrant. Yet, tyrants need people too. And that's why the Nazi Party and its members were so important to him. They were the native soil needed for the harvest of hate.

That harvest reached its fruition during the Great Blood Purge on June 30, 1934. On that fateful day, the innocent died along with the guilty. Loyal SA men along with Roehm; honorable military officers along with Schleicher. And all of this was the result of a power struggle within the party. Hitler had to choose between the SA (or the Brownshirts) and the army (or the Reichswehr). The Brownshirts and their murderous leader, Ernst Roehm, had helped Hitler attain power by controlling the streets of Germany and intimidating his political opponents. But, after Hitler was named Chancellor, he needed the support of the Reichswehr in order to continue his regime.

And the generals hated the SA and Roehm, who desired to replace the army. Hence, the dilemma and Hitler's solution could be predicted. In return for the generals' favor, he agreed to eliminate the SA on the last day of June.

It was a day of terror; thousands were arrested and shot. Roehm was first. He was given the choice of killing himself. When he refused, he was shot. Other SA leaders were not given a choice; they were immediately put in front of a firing squad. General Schleicher, the deceiver, was shot dead when he answered the door of his villa. When his wife stepped forward, she, too, was killed. By the way, I don't feel sorry for either one or for Roehm. Ernst was a brutal man, and on that day he learned that brutality knows no limits. And Schleicher was a sneak and an intriguer. They deserved to die. Others, however, merit more sympathy. Many were butchered from pure vengeance or for no good reason. Most were chosen arbitrarily. Despite what Hitler claimed days later, these murders did not enhance our national security. They were the beginning of an age of chaos. An age where nothing confronted nothingness.

As I say, there were many others who should not have died during the purge. Above all, this included that great embodiment of idealism, Gregor Strasser. Yes! I recall the first time I saw Strasser during my student days at the University of Munich in 1932. I remember those days as if it were a festival. I can still recall the cafes, the cream cakes, the acquaintances, the books and flowers—the sights, the smells, and the sounds of the good life. Ah, how quickly it would pass! Yes, I was a loner in those days, too; I loved to walk the streets accompanied only by my thoughts and dreams. How great it is to dream! In those days, I dreamed of noble things: good dreams for all mankind. How life deadens enthusiasm; how brutality crushes idealism! How great it is to dream! And how much greater is it to continue dreaming despite circumstances.

My dreams are dead! They died as a result of a specific event on a singular day. I remember that day well even though some twenty years have passed. It was a day in which I first encountered a Nazi street rally and slowly began a descent into hell. Gregor Strasser was just being introduced. I focused on his robust frame, his bulging eyes, and intense speech. I can still visualize the enthusiasm all around me that transformed by basic lack of ardor into exaltation. As Strasser began to speak, a portly worker ran up and handed me a pamphlet, which I glanced at intermittently. After a few perfunctory greetings, Strasser began to enunciate his program: the necessity to destroy the hated Versailles Treaty, to crush the communists, to kill the Jews, and to confiscate unearned wealth. I cheered every word as passion overwhelmed me—especially the part that called for the murder of the Jews. It all seemed so reasonable, so simple, and right! (Ah, how seriously I took such things in those days. Today, I could not care less! Let the nation collapse! Let the middle class collapse! For that matter, let mankind descend into nothingness!) And I mean that from the heart.

A few days later, I made one of the important decisions of my life: I joined the party. I cannot enumerate the reasons since they deal more with passion than with logic. Certainly, it was not because of some attraction to Hitler whose lowly social origins and crude nature repelled me. My attachment to him came later. Nor was it due to anti-Semitic motives. True, I despised Kozik, my only close university acquaintance, but this was from personal considerations. I hated his provincialism, his snobbishness, and his smell. Above all, I despised his devotion to the quest for brotherly love. (Yet, all in all, I was convinced that the Jews were a tolerable people.)

Rather, it was Strasser and the socialist idea that enticed me—ideas that the party left behind years ago. (Strasser, yes, to this day you bring back fond memories!) I certainly can say this about my decision: I joined the party to serve the interests of justice. Of course, the system came to symbolize the opposite, an injustice that has now turned against me.

These sobering reflections ceased with the emergence of one Mr. Dollard, a court appointed defense attorney. A shabbily dressed man in a dark suit with a narrow slit necktie, he greeted me formally and then, with more enthusiasm than sorrow, said that I would be tried for sedition the following Tuesday. I responded with agitation, "Sedition, for what reason?"

"For teaching works that the Propaganda Ministry deemed offensive," he answered without emotion.

I queried: "What works?"

"Kozik for one. This despicable Jew is a traitor to the Fatherland. And you have been observed quoting the New Testament," he replied.

I interrupted: "Wait a minute. You must be fooling."

He continued to talk as his voice rose to a harsh tone: "Do you think I would be here if we were fooling? Mr. Sovare, you are facing serious charges. Your fate is in Judge Freisler's hands. I recommend that you be apologetic."

"What of my record of service to the party?" I retorted.

"It is noted," he acknowledged with hesitation. "You are a transplanted Englishman, are you not?"

"So was Houston Stewart Chamberlain, one of the great prophets of our movement," I rebutted.

He finally said, "I am not trying to put you on the defensive, but simply noting the facts. Here is a summary of the charges. Again, I recommend that you be apologetic."

After that, I was brought back to my cell. Some justice! Well, what can you expect from a creature as base— no, as sick—as man. Let's face it, history from the time of Hannibal proves only one thing: that nothing is just. And justice in the Third Reich was particularly despicable. In fact, positive law had ceased to exist—the law and the will of Hitler were one. Judges were appointed on the basis of party loyalty and misused their positions to punish the dictator's enemies. Verdicts were arbitrary, sentences were severe, and bribes were commonplace. The Gestapo, also, was the law. Only a rash person would dare seek justice within this system. The "kingdom of the arbitrary"—that's what it was! Yes, the kingdom of the arbitrary. Justice was whatever the Reich defined it to be.

In my case, that lack of integrity confined me to a cell—or should I say confined my body. My thoughts journeyed beyond this limited time and place to embrace both the world's and my own past. My notions focused on essences: those qualities of feeling and mind which imbue life with heartfelt meaning and profound emotional depth. The positive memory of being held in my mother's arms, the magnificence of my education, the mastery of the visual arts, and the enrichment of philosophy. While thinking of essences, I participate in eternity. My body may ebb, but my immutable essence remains. No doubt, I will die, but my essence shall endure. And so I thought.

However, despite these thoughts, or perhaps because of them, the shocking issues at hand continued to nauseate me. A web of lies! I had always lectured on the principle that a professor must pronounce the truth. While I did quote certain sources offensive to the Propaganda Ministry, my actions were basically within the state's dictates. Now, I don't say I've been truthful in most aspects of my life as I generally have no positive will to truth. Other people are my enemies! I don't owe them the courtesy of the truth. To the contrary, I have a positive obligation to mislead. (Ha, have I done this in this memoir?) My truth, the truth of my soul, will always remain a mystery. It will not be 'played upon,' but rather go with me to my grave.

And, come to think of it, how ironical it is that a quote from Kozik should be mentioned in the summary since I despise him. No, not because he was a Jew. I hated what he represented: humanity, cosmopolitanism and cowardice. Yes, he was a coward! Remember, in the early twenties, his was an important and influential voice, one that was needed in the fight against our dear Fuehrer. But, where was Kozik? How many times did he risk his personal safety? Millions of Germans were deceived by Hitler, but Kozik saw the truth from the beginning and did nothing. Remember Burke's famous dictum: the only thing necessary for the triumph of evil is that good men do nothing. Anyway, Kozik was not a good man. He was one of those liberal swine who do not have the courage of their convictions. Hitler did have that type of courage. Say anything you want about him, but you must admit this much: he had the courage to die for his ideas. During the Great War, he was a brave soldier. He continually jeopardized his personal safety during personal appearances. And, in the end, he put a bullet through his right temple rather than dishonorably surrender. Compare this behavior to Kozik's, a man obsessed with his academic prerogatives and leisures. And in merry old London with the whores and raving dogs, where you can urinate on any prostitute at will. (Oh, how I loved to urinate on whores!) The Fuehrer, I'm afraid, was more concerned with the consolidation of power in Germany.

Also, I'm tired of the sacrosanct position Earlstein has nowadays—as if he's above criticism. As if his intellectual accomplishments justify every aspect of his life. As if he didn't defecate! Remember, this was the man who helped develop weapons of mass destruction during the Second World War. While he later regretted it, his responsibility for the hundreds of thousands of deaths that ensued remains unchanged. Also, recall this: after he was expelled, he urged the development of these weapons against his own country. And this constituted treason. His should have been the fate of Quisling—infamy!

The other reference for which I was called to account concerned Jesus of Nazareth. I admit quoting New Testament narrative, but only to note an important philosophical truth, namely, that Christ did *not* share the true existential passion of man. He had one absolute assurance that no other human being ever possessed: he had total certainty concerning the existence of God, whose divinity he shared. He never had any doubt concerning the significance of his own life or mission. He infallibly knew that there was a moral structure to the world. He never had to agonize over the profound metaphysical mysteries that plague all of us. He shared only the physical side of human suffering, not the more profound spiritual aspect. He never feared that a mere accident would relegate him to obscurity; he knew his star was firmly wedged in the scheme of things and that the trash and garbage of civilization would never overtake him. Having the assurance of ultimate triumph, he could never know the inner darkness that comes from the suspicion that one is a lost soul. Or, even worse, that one has no soul—that one is only a breakable animal. To be a mere cipher; to be at the periphery of the dust; to be on the wrong side of history; to be unwanted by any living person; to be a mere toilet for slaves; and to be unfulfilled at the end of life—here and here alone does one fully grasp the meaning of futility. This is the torment that eluded Christ. Yet, this is the fate of Bertrand Sovare. I would rather bear the torture of a thousand crosses than endure this life of idleness without meaning or hope or joy.

If the Heavenly Father had really wanted Christ to share our human agony, he should have blocked from his memory all knowledge of his divine origin and allowed him to search fruitlessly for an oasis of meaning in this nihilistic desert. He should have inflicted on him the same moral dilemmas that plague us all; he should have allowed him to search in vain for evidence of design; he should have permitted him to perform good only to receive evil in return—and with no hope of ultimate transcendence or eventual vindication; he should have then allowed his life efforts to amount to nil—merely to come so close to the grave that he could view the ignominy of dust; he should have restricted his choices to the bad and the worst—both being conductive to practical ends, yet neither offering redemption; above all, he should have inflicted upon him the same monotonous economic routines imposed on millions of others where puny tasks must be completed every day for no reason other than money. And if awakened from this agonized dream of life with a full awareness of his divine inheritance, he might then have a true understanding of the futility of existence. Might he finally, as I did, have drawn the proper conclusion? Would he hate this miserable world with its vain hopes and veil of tears and in one final great act of divine omnipotence will it out of existence? And so I thought and lectured my classes. And so I now pondered. This tired me and I rested on my narrow cot. I glanced briefly at the alternating shades of light and darkness on the walls. I then fell asleep.

It was not a refreshing sleep, but one of unsettling dreams. I hate dreams, those alternative worlds of darkness and perversion. In my dreams, I drink urine and eat feces. I do not recall this directly, but I have intimations. I have always had a fascination with my stools. Perhaps my excrement provides me with hints of death for it is none else, as Schopenhauer wrote, but flesh that had died or a form of perpetual perishing. Also, I must confess: I love to urinate in improper places! My obsession with urine negates all my attempts to live "normally." In dreams I descend from this rational bourgeois world into a pit of diarrhea, sweat, and saliva. I can then awaken unscathed and play my part—the role of professor—or whatever other mask I happen to fancy. I can again play the game of pleasure and pain or pretend to advocate good middle class morality. I was, after all, until recently a decent bourgeois. Those around me, however, never knew the dreams that enmesh me in a world of diarrhea. Enough! I cannot stand these thoughts!

Yet, there must be something I enjoy about them since I recall certain memories fondly. In merry old England—or, perhaps, merrie olde England, to capture the medieval spelling—I loved to urinate on English whores: Claire, for instance! As a former friend, I invited her to lunch. I then quickly lifted her worn bra and bit continuously on her right nipple. Dear old Claire seemed to enjoy this until I held her down against her will and urinated on her chest. What a joy! Claire ran away like a defiled bitch. A chipmunk dripping with kidney fluid. Oh, the lovely memories of my native land!

What really occupied me was a dream that I had the night before. It filled me with a sense of unreality, a weird feeling that made me question the veracity of what was before me. I felt like a marginal person, as if I existed between two worlds. In the dream, I confronted two armed men standing near a doorway. One was short, the other was oversized. Suddenly, as I approached, they began firing. In a panic, I ran to an adjacent cemetery and hid amidst the memorials and tombstones. In a sense, it seemed real. But, somehow I knew the cemetery was artificial, as if I didn't belong there. Yet, in a manner, I did. It was home. Later, upon awakening, a feeling of ambivalence terrified me and produced an eerie sense of uncertainty. It also made me wonder just how rational any mind could be, which is at night the scene of such fantasies and perversions.

I then sat up with anticipation. The waiting was unbearable; when would these people have the decency to inform me about my situation? No, they would rather have me sit here as a vegetable! My hatred of the culture around me grew with each passing day. What a monstrous culture the German culture has become! Why, oh why, have the Germans never become civilized? Other European cultures have risen above the brute forces of nature. But, then again, the Germans were unique. Several distinct steps led to their descent into barbarism. The first and perhaps most important occurred almost two thousand years ago. In 9 A.D. a Roman army under Publius Quintilius Varus, a new Roman governor, reached the Germanic lands. His three legions were part of a force that had conquered the known world from Baetica to Thracia. And they had every expectation of further victory. Caesar Augustus, the emperor, had so ordered, and Varus was determined. However, Arminius, a Germanic tribal leader, waited in secret with a small but determined force. He knew that there was no chance of defeating the Romans in the open field; he must sabotage them as they marched through the rough country. Then he attacked in the forest amidst the rain, mud, and wind. The Romans were overwhelmed and rendered incapable of using their superior forces. They tried to retreat to their nearest fortress, Aliso. But even here they failed. Within three days, except for a few who escaped under cover of darkness, they were all dead. And with them died the dream of a Latinized Germania. As Hitler later did, Varus died by his own hand rather than surrender. (This

I admire! Suicide is better than dishonor! Take a blade to your enemies or yourself rather than die at the hands of crass executioners or dank physicians. The latter are the worst!) In any case, Caesar never recovered from this blow. His walked around his palace for years saying, "Quintilius Varus, give me back my legions!" Rome was shaken as it was never before. Due of this event, Germany was never unified under Roman rule and remained an outcast nation developing quite separate folkways and mores—customs and morals that rendered that nation uncivilized. Gone was a potential legacy of literature, architecture, art, law, and government. In its place, barbarian culture reigned supreme!

That culture remained bifurcated for almost two thousand years until Chancellor Bismarck unified it by force in a series of wars, including the one that defeated Austria. This baptism in blood created a nation where the exercise of military prowess became the supreme achievement of Germanic man. So it was under Kaiser Wilhelm II during the Great War and later under Adolf Hitler. Due to this emphasis on force, the legitimacy of the state was seldom based on positive law, but rather on charismatic personalities; that is, the rightful exercise of state authority was based on great personal talents or qualities of the leader instead of constitutions and charters. Bismarck's legitimacy was based on his personal skill, both diplomatic and organizational. Hitler's was based on his oratorical ability and political cunning. Never was the law the basis of his power. Hence, the law and the will of Hitler were one.

This lack of positive law led to a complete denial of freedom and privacy. There were hundreds of thousands of informants working for the Secret State Police or the Gestapo. Since there were only eighty million Germans, this meant one informant for every few hundred people. This was the ultimate police state: every action, every word, every gesture came under close scrutiny. Attacking Hitler or criticizing any policy of the state could lead to a knock at the door in the middle of the night. And that invariably led to severe beatings, torture, or a trip to Dachau. No one could trust anyone else. Your neighbor might be working for the SS. Or, perhaps, your son. It was like living in the age of the witch hunts hundreds of years ago. In the southern Germanic lands, several thousand women were convicted of witchcraft—they were supposedly possessed by Satan or were seen in two places at one time. They died by burning or mutilation. And for what reason? Is there a deep, genetic need in the German people to hunt and murder or an uncontrolled lust for blood? Are the Germans central European marauders? Possibly! More likely, however, this type of behavior was an attempt to explain away personal or societal misfortunes. The cause of the Black Death in the late Middle Ages was little understood. If someone died, it seemed that a witch was responsible. In the same way, a famine could be blamed on witchcraft. How convenient! In 1918, Germany was defeated in the Great War. The Nazis preached that Germany did not surrender, but was stabbed in the back by unsavory Jews at home. By killing the Jew, said Hitler, we do the work of the Lord. As in the case of the witch, this savagery ensured the general prosperity.

In either case, I do not believe that our modern police state was accidental. It was the result of biological, social, and historical factors that go back hundreds, if not thousands, of years. It is almost in the makeup of the German people to be this way. We always seem to be on witch hunts. Jung, of course, believed that there are inherited patterns of thought or archetypes that are transmitted genetically. Symbols, you might say, which are handed down by our genes. The crooked cross is certainly one. It was not invented by Hitler. This symbol is one of the oldest emblems on this planet. I myself have seen it in books on ancient Mesopotamian civilizations. Hitler probably saw it somewhere in Austria or Bavaria and appropriated it for himself. But it took considerable genius to choose it since it inspires awe, loyalty, and fear at a single glance. It is a symbol to die for. And the same is true of the Nazi salute. This was originally a Roman innovation. Yet, its archetypal element is no accident. To pledge loyalty under our flag to Adolf Hitler was to salute a god, a Teutonic deity. The great issues of life are formed more by our genes than by our whims. And Hitler was the fulfillment of our deepest urges.

The history of German philosophy provided the final cause or, as I should say, the slanted nature of German thinking. The German thinkers of the nineteenth century created a spiritual break from other Western philosophical traditions. The philosophy of a nation defines the symbols of that race. Our race did produce Leibniz and Kant, two of the greatest minds in history. But our thinking in the past two centuries rested more on Hegel, Schopenhauer, Nietzsche, and Fichte. Although his metaphysics was one of the greatest of all time, Hegel often extolled the supremacy of the state over the individual. And he glorified the Germanic idea as absolute. Schopenhauer's philosophy demonstrates great wisdom. Yet, he did emphasize the primacy of will over reason and the irrational evil in every man. Man was a savage. "Man the beast," as Dr. Goebbels later correctly said. And the great philosopher, for all his cunning, did disparage the rights of women, perhaps with some justification. (I love his remark that a woman is an intermediate stage between a child and a fully grown man.) Nietzsche was a genius, but the unbalanced nature of his mind is reflected in every page. (The Germans must be "lords of the earth." he wrote—a favorite phrase of Hitler.) He glorified the will to power in human relations. And Fichte was as ardent a nationalist as Heidegger later was a dedicated Nazi. Some may think me wrong, but I do believe that the ideals and behavior of the great can filter down to the level of the common man. Alfred Adler once said that a person's behavior was derived from their ideas. And, of course, the ideas of the great are further distorted from erroneous interpretation by lesser thinkers such as Dietrich Eckart and Alfred Rosenberg. The latter, the so- called philosopher of Nazism, was the most odious. His racial theories were considered laughable except, no doubt, by the majority of the Nazis who regarded them as sacrosanct. The former was no more than a drunken poet. The result could be seen in the collective mind. It was lethal—the foundation of the New Order and the mind of Hitler. He once said, "We are barbarians. We want to be barbarians. It is an honorable title." Whether it is just or unjust, this was the fruition of the German mind.

Enough of this dissertation! Maybe, I should redirect my mind and think of something positive, something to uplift my spirits. But, what?

Incredible, isn't it? In this so-called best of all possible worlds, I can't think of a single thing. Not one! Perhaps, the beauty of the natural world? Yes, years ago, when I was a Lutheran, I appreciated the order and stability of the moral and physical world. As the Bible says, God has revealed himself in the things he has made. Things he made before man and beings that are beyond the understanding of man. Wonders that impress us with a sense of the overwhelming, with a sense of awe. But, here again, my education interferes. (You know, sometimes it's best to be simple; life then presents few problems.) In this regard, I think of the famous remark: nature is beautiful to look at, but dreadful in reality. A forest may be scenic, yet half the forest may be destroying the other half in the struggle for survival. And in exactly what way is it scenic anyway? I laugh at those who extol flowers as beautiful, as if they were designed to evoke aesthetic responses in man. The truth, I'm afraid, is more prosaic. Plant colors and images evolved for the eyes of insects who alone can discern their patterns in order to facilitate pollination. Yet, men continue to laud vegetation as a spontaneous expression of natural beauty. (As if five billion years of evolution could have had no loftier purpose than to be aesthetically pleasing to the "sick species.") Not to belabor the point, but I'm sure this scenic beauty was in full bloom when millions were being murdered at the hands of Himmler. Some compensation, is it not?

Ah, maybe I should think of something else. Perhaps the great works of man, material culture: de Chirico's metaphysical paintings, Beethoven's music, or the writings of Johann Wolfgang Goethe. Might not these magnificent achievements provide me with values to live by? Possibly! As most scholars, I believe ideas are more real than material things—we are all Plato's disciples in this regard. Great ideas, in specific, allow us to live in a world of gods who create and dispose at will. Spinoza's universe is an intellectual world of the first magnitude, as was Kant's. Yet, this world of enduring satisfaction cannot negate the mundane realities that seem to engulf most of us. Let's face it, I've been a dedicated academician all my life. And how am I improved by it? I must still live in this base world and suffer the indignities. Can all the great classics atone for that? Can the baseness of the great mass be redeemed by the achievements of the few? Hardly! Every great insight could never compensate for life's one overpowering truth—that man is vile. A sick ape lying, cheating, and excreting! A gorilla that dreams of god! (Yes, I hope this species becomes extinct. It is my one true wish for mankind.) And what is culture anyway but a mask for brutality? We murder millions in death camps and then praise ourselves for reading Goethe and Hegel. Yes, Goering was right! Culture is hateful. Every time I hear the word culture, I too reach for my revolver.

And people? How could they enliven me? I know very few people—few whom I really like—even fewer whose company I enjoy. During my university days, I had numerous acquaintances, yet in my heart I hated them. My nature was not always this way; I once was open, sociable, and morally correct. It is as if that person had died—perhaps as a result of brutality and selfishness. (You know, it's impossible to know the moral worth of a person without understanding his circumstances.) Later in life, I looked at nearly everyone as a potential enemy. I greeted my colleagues only for official purposes and felt nothing afterwards; often, I would wish them dead when they walked away. I also cared little for my students. I lectured on Heraclitus and then regretted inspiring them personally or academically. More and more, I began to compare myself to the great minds of philosophy rather than to my compatriots. I lived increasingly in a world of abstractions, devoid of individuals or events or humanity. I had no friends. Not one! My memories were malignant; hence, I refused to contact anyone who would remind me of them. In the end, even my dedication to teaching was little more than a patronizing attempt to demonstrate my professional vigor to myself. I hated teaching and abhorred the idea of improving the minds of the young. You know, I would rather have been a great destroyer. Attila, the "Scourge of God." (Yes! Glory amid the ruins!) No doubt, there is a heartfelt fulfillment in destruction, a massive inner satisfaction that expresses contempt and hatred for life. (Here lies the real reason why I joined the party: for in this hatred I share a common mind with Hitler.) My God, how I choose the wrong profession! How I wish that I could murder millions!

Given my preference, I would choose the fate of General Paulus at Stalingrad, surrounded by Russians and ordered by Hitler to defend the city to the last man. Paulus failed in this historic mission. He weakened! He did not have the moral courage necessary to the task. The Sixth Army should have fought with greater fanaticism, and Paulus should have shot himself with his last bullet. What a disgrace that surrender was. On February 2, 1943, nearly one hundred thousand German soldiers, including twenty-four generals, went into captivity. It was the greatest defeat in our history.

Hitler was rightfully outraged. Even a promotion to field marshal had not strengthened Paulus's resolve. What a disgrace! Hitler shouted: "Even Varus gave his slave the order: 'Now kill me!'" Yes, one must know when and how to die. Hitler knew how to do this. In defending Berlin to the last, the Fuehrer set an example that will go down in the history of the ages. Paulus's only legacy was his cowardice. It's pitiful that historic moments are squandered by inferior men. Great men live on in mythology. Along with Caesar Augustus and Napoleon Bonaparte, Hitler remains one of the most written about men in history and popular culture. In movies and on television, the masses remain fascinated with this man, his ideas, and his movement. And, above all, in America, which was his greatest enemy. Hitler had predicted, in his last will and testament, that the "seed will be sown that will grow...to the glorious rebirth of the National Socialist movement." Truly, the more things change, the more they remain the same!

My mind then again quickly descended to my immediate problems, which included being confined to my cell during this period of my detainment. Yet, once in a while, I was escorted by SS guards to and from the various court buildings. Court officials would ask for more and more and more information; the process was endless. Nonetheless, it occasionally gave me the opportunity to go outdoors and glance at the skies or the heavens. It is easy to become entangled in our petty affairs and ignore the dimensions above. And how small man seems compared to those magnitudes. The colors of the firmament, the seeming images in the clouds, and the brilliance of the stars have often evoked in me intimations of a creator. As if beyond all this petty strife, there could be a larger purpose, an aim beyond all our foregone hopes or dreams. Perhaps even a transcendent being—Christ! Yes or no? Nah! In my heart, I really don't believe this. I know better. Intellect interferes with the desires of the heart. What is the whole truth? The design of the world is an illusion and that glorious human destiny only an absurdity. (This world is the result of a primordial catastrophe beyond any we could possibly imagine.) And man's dominance here is a result of his predatory nature, which also ends in his destruction. The ascent of man was a natural process, and so will be his descent.

CHAPTER FIVE

The days passed into weeks; the weeks seemingly into months. Upon arrival, I fully expected a swift execution of my trial. I had little doubt that it would result in my death. Yet, nothing happened!

The delays were endless; my lawyer was no where to be found; the interrogations seemed purposeless. Also, the food was scarce, and all diversions were denied me. I was again alone with my thoughts. One thought, in particular, obsessed me: a dream image of an open sewer in which I was submerged. I thought of that often. My dream was truthful—my life had become a sewer. A sewer of loneliness; a sewer of indignities. The loneliness was like an eternal silence, a cold silence. That silence was occasionally interrupted by a few peripheral contacts. Frequently, those contacts brought news.

The one momentous item of news was the announcement of the army's attempt to murder Hitler. It was a report that would assume an awesome significance as the summer progressed since it soon initiated a grotesque sequence of events which would lead to the death of thousands of innocent people. It sealed my fate! Many of those who died were strangled by piano wire suspended from meat hooks; others were hunted down like rabid dogs or sent to detention camps; the remainder were simply shot. The assassination attempt did not surprise me. I had always believed that only the armed forces possessed the brute force necessary to overthrow the Nazi regime.

Certainly neither the Gestapo nor the SD could ever move against Hitler—even assuming that they had the will, which they did not. They were organs of the party. Even the so-called conspirators were a small group of isolated men with limited power. This left the murderous task to the army, the only branch of the armed forces that really counted, and the German General Staff. The latter, composed of the elite Junker class, was before 1933 a state within a state, subject to no authority but itself.

Even after Hitler's rise to power, it had never fully come under the party's auspices. Several of its prominent members hated the Fuehrer and for good reason: they were autocrats or former Junkers who despised Hitler's lowly social origins. In addition, they did not share his goals; most of them wanted a restoration of the old Hohenzollern monarchy. Also, while they wanted a strong Germany, they did not share Hitler's lust for extended conquest: *"Deutschland ueber Alles."* And Hitler knew this, but he had a dilemma. He could not simply eliminate them as he had with other political parties, the churches, or the labor unions. He needed them—their power, their discipline, and their military traditions—to carry out his vast plan of conquest throughout Europe. True, he had the SA, or People's Army, yet this group of swine lacked the might or internal organization necessary to carry out extensive military operations. So he had to coexist with this Junker body. They continued to reject Nazi ideology and served as a citadel of power that defied him.

Now, this in no way means that they acted against him swiftly or with moral righteousness. To the contrary, they acted slowly, in almost a haphazard manner. In the beginning, many of the members were seduced by him; they embraced the idea of rebuilding the armed forces in defiance of the restrictions imposed by the Treaty of Versailles. Later, they were willing enough to cooperate as long as victory ensued from Poland to France. But, after the Russian invasion, terrible defeat followed. Then, after Stalingrad, disaster! It was this catastrophe that opened the eyes of the German General Staff; they decided to murder Hitler in order to save Germany. Or so they later said. I say they decided to save themselves! (How many times have men tried to justify their own selfishness by wearing the mask of altruism?)

In any case, on July 20, 1944, they finally acted. Count Von Stauffenberg placed a bomb only a few feet from the Fuehrer's legs during a regular military conference. The blast resembled the explosion of a 155mm. shell. Bodies flew out of the room amid the debris; rubble fell far and wide. Stauffenberg was certain that Hitler was dead and conveyed that impression via telephone to the conspirators in Berlin. Appearances were, however, tragically deceptive. Several innocent men were decapitated, such as the stenographer and General Korten. Yet, in this world that the theologians keep telling us was created by an all-good, all-powerful God, Hitler survived the explosion! He was momentarily impaired, but not severely injured. In fact, within a few hours, he was again ordering the death of a wide spectrum of civilians. Hitler's survival doomed the plot since the conspirators could no longer count on the wavering generals and other party leaders who otherwise might have supported them. Men of courage always pay a price and most of these conspirators suffered a gruesome death by strangulation. The Fuehrer said that they must die like cattle—and they did, by piano wire suspended from meat hooks. Their death agony was filmed to be later shown as a warning.

Somehow, Hitler always seemed to escape assassination, and he survived this time too. It was as if some sort of an evil god protected him, an arbitrary god of power. (Or perhaps the Satan of Scripture.) As I think of it now, the end of the conspirators was inevitable as soon as it became known that he would live. His status was above the touch of any profane hand; his charisma guaranteed that. Moreover, the rank and file of the officers were bound to him by an oath of allegiance. Hitler, a man of no conscience, was a genius at creating strong obligations in the minds of inferior men. These alliances now ensured his tenure. This was an immense tragedy. If he had been assassinated on that day, the war almost certainly would have ended a year earlier. In that remaining year, more people were killed than in the preceding five. Europe was laid waste, and Germany was overrun by the bowlegged Russians. Of course, during all of this, God remained idle. What a useless deity! Even I, a misanthrope, almost weep when I think of Count Von Stauffenberg, who was shot during the abortive attempt. (Indeed, on the day before his mission, he is said to have stopped at a Christian cathedral to pray for divine assistance—in vain as it turned out.) The Heavenly Father had already decreed Stauffenberg's death, not Hitler's. The facts must be faced. History is only the sum of blind forces, abortive dreams and deplorable purposes. And even if it wasn't, it would make little difference anyway. It wouldn't change the past. No being can do that—not even God if he exists.

You know, I sometimes make myself laugh when I revert to my petty bourgeois morality. I often hope an asteroid destroys this planet, and now

I pretend to bemoan the death of one decent man. Certainly, I'm not above hypocrisy. As if hypocrisy wasn't essential to life itself! Who could be expected to believe everything that was asserted in the course of even one day? When someone says hello to you, you must hello in return. But, do you always mean it? A greeting from me is merely functional. I really mean to say one thing: drop dead! Yet, at a more basic level, there is a decency in me that all of these adverse circumstances have not destroyed. A basic kernel of goodness that illuminates this benighted being. A very strange man you are, Bertrand Sovare. Strange, yes; strange, indeed! All men are to some degree strangers to themselves, and all men show contradictions in the course of their daily lives. I'm no different. My moral proclivities relate to specific social settings. As these change, so do my moral judgments. In one setting, I may encounter a friend who communicates some profound grief. I then express a genuine and heartfelt sympathy. But, an hour later, I may react with total indifference upon hearing of the death of ten thousand strangers. (Why should I be squeamish when informed of the mass death of strangers? And I assure you, I am not! In fact, I relish it.) Yet, I really must not be too harsh on myself. In other situations, I have been kind and sympathetic. Nay, even humble. (And how I smile at that!) But, then again, I shouldn't grin too broadly. This malignant will, which turns on me without anchor or direction, was once a benevolent volition that recognized the higher purposes of the true God. Yes, years ago in England, I accepted the will of God in a straightforward, sincere, and simple manner. I had befriended a group of Christians who led me to God's word by faith and friendship. They taught me to believe in one God—total, good, transcendent, and above human failings. They taught me to see his order and law in the universe. And they answered my most profound questions in a way that I had never before conceived. They informed me that disobedience to God's law is a matter of the will, not the intellect. That those who reject God's law, as given to Moses, do not want the true God to interfere in their lives. So they rationalize or make excuses to justify their lack of faith. Evolution, the evil of the world, unexplained mysteries, the rise of science, the hypocrisy of the churches, or the improbability of miracles. It all comes down to one thing: willful desire to disobey the true Creator of the universe. Evolution, for example. Who really cares what happened millions or billions of years ago? A few impotent scientists perhaps. Yet, most atheists give this as a reason for disbelieving the story of Adam and

Eve in Genesis. As if they really cared. Evolution, by the way, is not a new theory; it is one of the oldest of man's ideas. I myself have seen this theory in ancient Hindu scripture and in the writings of Anaximander of Miletus, who lived about 2500 B.C. He said that the first living beings were born from moisture and evolved into a different type of creature later. Darwin gave evolution a modern form and provided a great deal of empirical evidence to document it—evidence that is not believed by scientists today, for modern evolutionary ideas are based largely on genetics that pertain more to plant and insect life. The general public accepts evolution because it is an attempt to explain creation without a creator, a goal they desired before they learned of that theory.

The theory is spurious. It might pertain to lower forms of life or possibly even to changes in man as time goes on, but it does not explain certain facts—for example, that man is the only creature who can think by symbols that do not resemble the object they refer to. A dog can learn the meaning of the word *food*. but he cannot learn the meaning of freedom or the meaning of the concept *mind*. Yet, man's brain is no larger than that of many other animals. It also does not explain the emergence of complex organs such as the eye. Yet, the newer theory of the Christ does explain this: that man was given a divine mind by the creator God and that this mind is not explainable by any physical process and that its categories cannot be reduced to any material form. The body itself was designed by God. Hence, the emergence of such complex organs as the eye. These Christians pounded into my mind the notion that evolution is an atheist's attempt to explain away the Heavenly Father.

And the evil of the world? They suggested to me that this is because most people do not worship the true God. If we did worship him, these horrible occurrences would be eradicated. The first parents, Adam and Eve, were given a divine mind, and they disobeyed the law of God; hence, the expulsion from Eden. When I protested that I could not believe this, they asked me why. I said that it went against logical scientific belief. They answered: "God's law does not have to be understood scientifically, but accepted as the divine revelation of the Christ." "Trust Christ," they continued. "Believe in his divine judgment, and you will always land on high ground." I thought deeply. Even Schopenhauer argued that the one myth in scripture he respected was that of Adam and Eve. He had always believed that this world order had started with some primeval error, some great mistake or some ancient "falling away" for which we are all atoning today. Perhaps this is the ultimate reason for the horror of the Third Reich. Man was created to live in an open relationship with the true God. Under Hitler, we freely chose the way of destruction and death. Our god was Adolf Hitler.

My Christian brothers and sisters, also, had other answers to my concerns and doubts. In fellowship, I gave and took freely from them—and, above all, from God. Seeking guidance and help, I appealed to God in crisis and in merriment. And I received the good bounty. During this time in my life, I was fulfilled. But then my mind turned inward, and I thought of petty grievances. I concentrated on the few areas of my life that were unfulfilled and ignored the infinite riches of Christ. And I was consumed with despair. After all, my spiritual walk obligated me to obey the one above. Yet, my will had always been prime and it would be so again. I rationalized every step away from God. (I thought constantly of biblical contradictions and unnecessary evils. I read Freud and Nietzsche to the near exclusion of all else.) My natural inclinations then reemerged—my drunkenness, my gambling, my sexual perversions and my obesity. I again became a child of sin, and there I remain. I also became increasingly sure that my choices were right. That soon led to conviction.

Enough! I now badly needed sleep. And my thoughts temporarily submerged into unconsciousness. Once again, my dreams gave me an eerie feeling, or perhaps a weird feeling, which emerges in that region between our common world and sleep. (A world devoid of common memories. A universe excluded from a sense of the familiar, almost as in a de Chirico painting.) In my dreams, I am walking and looking in the windows of shops, empty shops. Markets with neither merchants nor merchandise, streets with neither people nor personality. But they are definitely the same marts that I've dreamed of before. It makes me wonder if these images are really in my mind or are rather the fabric of some other flesh and blood world. (Oh, the hell with all this. I can barely understand my daily life. Forget about dreams!)

Suddenly, a guard stood before my cell. He opened it and his stern glance momentarily fixated upon me. "Come forward," he yelled. I needed to know why, but I was too weary to even make the effort. Anyway, what was the use? Without hesitation, I meekly walked down the narrow corridor to a dim, sparsely furnished room.

A stocky man in a dark suit sat behind the desk. I could barely see his face among the shadows. "I am Dr. Weissmann," he said with a combination of hesitation and agitation. "I have been appointed by Judge Freisler to conduct your defense."

I interrupted abruptly, "Dr. Weissmann. I have been brought here for no apparent reason. I have been held against my will. I demand an explanation."

"Calm down, sir," Weissmann firmly replied as his left fist pounded down on the desk. "I am here to answer your queries. I shall first need some background information. You are being charged with high treason."

I sat mute; my face turned to stone.

"This case revolves," he continued gamely, "around your duties at the university."

I insisted: "What duties?"

He answered directly: "Before revealing this, I need some additional information."

My face became agitated and I again asked in defiance, "What duties?" I then began to rise.

"Sit down," he commanded with a savage expression. I could clearly see his face. Rough features! Quite grotesque. No doubt, the sort of person I would avoid if given a choice. He resumed; "Surely, Mr. Sovare, you realize that your business in Munich did not always conform to accepted doctrine. You have discussed foreign ideas, ideas derived from Marx, Freud, Darwin, Einstein, and other Jew bums or assorted scum."

I could no longer control my anger: "This is pure nonsense!"

He responded abruptly: "Wait! Listen to what I am saying. I am here, after all, to help you. You fail to understand the gravity of the charges. The 1933 revolution has resulted in an eruption of German patriotism—a civic pride in our heritage—and that national feeling is now being undermined. Do you recall the beastly state of affairs before the Fuehrer? Evil stars surrounded us! Mass unemployment! Universal starvation! Bread lines and soup kitchens in every village in the land! We were a nation disarmed! A faltering nation! This has now all changed. This last decade has seen a solid resurgence in German mastery. We are in the midst of a celebration of German culture."

"I am quite willing to grant this," I hastily interjected, "but what has this to do with this case?"

"Look here," he bellowed with displeasure, "we are on the same side. You are acting as if I am your enemy. I am not your enemy. And, for that matter, the state is not your enemy. You are your own worst enemy based on your eccentric ideas and your simple inability to understand our revolution. "Our civilization embodies traditions that have evolved over centuries, and your ideas are inconsequential compared to this. We are not interested in your comments but rather in a nation conditioned by German blood. A universal culture is a mongrel culture, a development from half- breeds. So you see that your ideas are not benign; they are malignant."

I remained speechless for a moment in being immersed with puzzlement and disdain. I finally spoke: "This is all a matter of arbitrary interpretation."

He responded fiercely: "Once again, you fail to understand the magnitude of these charges. Quoting Freud, Buber, and Einstein—all Jews and traitors at that—does not appear to be a case based on arbitrary interpretation but rather on specific evidence which can be certified."

I could bear no more. I rose slowly, yet with resolution. Without attempting to hold back my indignation, I pointed my index finger at Weissmann and said: "I was interested in their philosophical ideas, not in their political agenda or even less their race."

"The two cannot be separated," he responded with increasing agitation. "You must remember that they are Jews; their ideas are destructive. Do you want generations of German children to learn Jew science? Remember, as is the case in all other human endeavors, science is conditioned by blood. Psychology and Freud—Jew science! Einstein and physics—Jewish physics! Dogs, bums, and scum !"

"This is preposterous," I raged, "I only cited their ideas for purposes of intellectual discussion."

He rebuffed this coldly: "We are not interested in intellectual discussion. This was invented by the Jews. We want blind obedience and absolute determination to carry out the will of the Fuehrer. Adolf Hitler is Germany, and Germany is Adolf Hitler. This is the only knowledge you need."

"Dr. Weissmann," I queried with intense weariness, "where did you receive your education?"

This evoked another savage expression; "You are not here to ask questions! I am now starting to see you as you really are. You are a Jew, either in blood or in spirit. Are you not?"

"I am a Lutheran," I said meekly.

"No, a Jew! A Jew who is going to die. Your interview is terminated."

I vehemently protested, but to no avail. He promptly summoned an SS functionary, and I was hastily brought back to my cell. I was now more confused than ever. And I was afraid. I could expect no help from this counsel. I was on my own.

CHAPTER SIX

Man is a breakable animal—breakable, indeed! When I think back to my early days and ideals, I find it inconceivable that I could ever have experienced an impasse such as this. Yet, here I am! I truly hate this world of flesh, this carnal earth. In it, every splash of blood affronts me. Oh, God, how I hate it so. Yes, how I hate it so! This is why I could never fully embrace God: I cannot accept his creation. Who could love that gory behemoth? To love God is as easy as to adore perfection; the mere thought of his bleeding children, however, is repulsive. The eternal Christ commands us to love; yet, I hate! A hatred so great that it negates everything; a malice so cosmic that it envelopes worlds. Every corner of my life is poisoned with disdain. I exist in a bottomless pit of excrement.

If only I had handled things differently, I should have cherished brotherhood. No, I have never valued that! I have always eluded people and, for that matter, never had a positive desire to engage in any human enterprise. I now have no one! Ultimately, the reason for this lies not in the world, but in me. There has always been a basic lack of joy in my life and a futile passion for solitude. A solitary atom! During my youth every avenue was nearly vacant. Hence, my isolation sheltered me from being reminded of this void.

In that void, I see only feces and urine. As I say, I have always been fascinated with my own excrement. I urinate in cans. And for that matter everywhere on an ongoing basis: in sinks, plates, doors , halls, and walls.

How I love urine! Perhaps, all life was created from it. Indeed, I call it the first principle of all things. Man was not created from above or from the purity of the heavens, but was rather the harvest of excrement. Yes, an inferior deity urinated and created this world! And I am its main derivative!

I tried to think of other things, but it was difficult. Waiting in my cell was unbearable. And even more so because of the bombings—the Americans came by day and the British by night—leaving us with no respite. Occasionally, I would come by an old newspaper, from the Nazi controlled press, of course, which meant its veracity could be questioned. In one, I read of an Allied air attack on Munich on July 13, 1944. Twelve hundred bombers and seven hundred fighters destroyed the city in two days. The fact that they were reporting these disasters was a clear sign that the end was near.

How uncivilized the world has become! War used to involve only professional armies. Today, whole populations are decimated, civilians and all. Leave it to the "sick species" to pervert the age of aviation. (You know, I wish the Wright Brothers had been assassinated. All we have done with this invention is allow the very rich to go quickly from point A to point B. Other social classes rarely fly, and, if they did, it wouldn't be important. The main use of this invention has been to destroy and destroy and destroy. (I know someone would have invented it sooner or later, but at least the pillage would have been delayed.)

In any case, I could hear the bombings night and day, especially since I was detained in Berlin. And that city was also in rubble. (In despair, I looked inward and thought of nothingness, the total void of being or the negation of my life. Normally, my daily routines prevented me from confronting this void. I was too busy to notice that everything was really nothing, so I could continue playing the games I played. Doctor, brother, professor, and so on.

Masks and games, that's what my life was about. But being here in such circumstances enhanced these metaphysical encounters. And they were psychologically debilitating. Time and space were unreal, and so was my sense of self. What is the self anyway? A sum of memories derived from others? A series of reactions to pleasure and pain? Or is it an illusion, a short interval between the totality of being before birth and the return to that totality after death? Even in the case of Christ, before his birth, was he not Melchisedec? Perhaps time and space are unreal! Which leaves pure being and nothingness. They are the same. A state of existence devoid of physical confrontation is nothing. Pure being, nothingness, essences; yes, this is heaven! (The hell with harps and nuns and brothers and reformed whores. Heaven consists of pure essences!)

Once again, I tried to concentrate on the issues at hand. My problem with Dr. Weissmann could only be understood within the context of the perversion of education under Hitler. The essence of education is free inquiry, and this was impossible in 1944. The Nazi Party had a stranglehold over the entire educational process. The Adolf Hitler schools were controlled by the Hitler Youth as directed by an insignificant, impotent fool whose entire life embodied mediocrity: Baldur von Schirach. The universities were administered by the Reich Minister of Education, a mindless functionary of the party. The Civil Service Act of 1937, which regulated the teaching profession, ensured this. The great days of the German mind were long past. New textbooks were written; Nazi guidelines were approved. Soon they were offering courses in "racial science" and "selective breeding." Einstein, Franck, Haber, and Warburg soon left teaching, to be replaced by mindless fanatics or party hacks. I somehow survived in this madhouse. Teaching was my only talent and I performed well. I spoke English and German fluently, having been raised in England before my arrival in Munich.

I enjoyed the great classics in both languages. I stayed to myself, however, and perhaps this is how I survived as long as I did. I pretended to accept Nazi doctrine while ignoring it at other times, particularly when teaching philosophy. I never imagined that any state official would be interested in the lectures of such a low profile philosopher as myself. I forgot that I was living in a police state.

The whole question of what I was teaching was simple as far as I was concerned. I taught quality: the great books of mankind, books that are continuously readable for insight and enjoyment. Among these would be the works of Plato, Aristotle, Kant, Hume, Spinoza, Schopenhauer, Nietzsche, Mendel, Whitehead, Thales, and Wittgenstein. Apparently, however, the Nazi fools wanted me to teach the joys of blind obedience and Spartan martial training. Some education, right? But, this is what these Nazi fanatics wanted. And I had neither the power nor the inclination to change them or to make them see reason. I was at their mercy.

You must remember what a fanatic is: someone who has no balance in his thinking. Extremes that normal people avoid are desirable to him. He has a few principles upon which he fixes his star to the exclusion of so many others that contradict them. He tries to live in a uniform, one-dimensional manner as if he were an insect with a predetermined pattern of instincts. Hitler was such a man. And so were Himmler, Hess, Rosenberg and von Ribbentrop. You cannot reason with such men. You can only fight them.

The men around Hitler were the dregs of society. The world's greatest philosopher, Plato, recommended thousands of years ago that philosopher kings should rule the state. That is, those who attained the highest degree of wisdom. Hitler's Reich demonstrates exactly the opposite: the ascendency of the gutter or the rule of the lowest of the low. Not only were the men around Hitler ignorant, but they also were individuals of personal and moral debauchery. Clearly, the lowest were Julius Streicher and Hermann Esser. Julius Streicher was a sadist and an avid anti-Semite. He produced a pornographic newspaper that specialized in morbid details of Jewish sexual crimes and secret plots to destroy the peace of Europe. He loved to whip those he disagreed with. Despite all this, Hitler appointed this despicable man to the position of party boss of Franconia. And Hermann Esser was little more than a sexual blackmailer and a trouble-maker. Others at this level of debauchery were a wrestler whose name I can't recall and Christian Weber, a bouncer and horse trainer. These were men of almost no administrative or personal ability.

One step above this scum were men who had some talent in certain limited areas but who clearly were not first rate. Here one could include Ernst Roehm, who was a skillful organizer of the SA, which played such a vital role in Hitler's rise to power, but who possessed a limited intellect and no moral qualities. Also, there was Heinrich Himmler, the former chicken farmer, who controlled the vast apparatus of the SS, which brought terror into the lives of so many millions. A mild mannered man, almost naive in certain ways, he was enormously indifferent to human suffering although he was not a sadist. He was somewhat of a crackpot, believing in all sorts of Aryan pseudoscientific theories and ideas. He was massively interested in Aryan origins and artifacts. At the end of the war, he betrayed Hitler and seems to have really believed that the Americans would appoint him the postwar ruler of Germany.

And, of course, there was Joachim von Ribbentrop, Hitler's foreign minister, whose arrogance and ignorance of foreign affairs became legendary. This individual who started life as a champagne salesman was one who generally looked at the world in terms of superiority and inferiority, or strength and weakness; life is too complex to be observed as such. Some observers thought Ribbentrop acted as if he owned Europe and Asia. He was inflexible and a notorious toady in Hitler's presence, which is possibly why he lasted as long as he did despite his incompetence. Even his greatest achievement, the Nazi-Soviet Pact in August 1939, was more Hitler's doing than his. He was little more than Hitler's puppet. He was despised by his peers, especially Goebbels, and even lost the confidence of Hitler by 1945.

The case of Hermann Goering is different. This greedy, fat associate of the German dictator was a man of considerable talent and administrative ability. As an air ace during the Great War and later commander-in-chief of the German Air Force, he became the number two Nazi after Hitler. He controlled the four-year plans regulating the economy and was essentially responsible for developing the concentration camps. He once boasted of having burned down the Reichtag. And he also gloated about the many millions who died in Russia by starvation in 1941. He would take the responsibility for bloodshed that would have unnerved even Hitler. He was, in addition, a drug addict and a lover of idle luxury—and art treasures plundered from priceless European collections. Toward the end of the war, he became slothful and incompetent. He often looked like a gigolo in a convalescent home. Hitler had no respect for him during the last days and ordered him arrested for treason.

And then there were the true believers: Paul Joseph Goebbels and Rudolf Hess. Both truly believed in Nazism and Adolf Hitler, without whose help neither would ever have been known to the world. Dr. Goebbels was an unsuccessful playwright and amateur novelist who found salvation in Hitler. His talent was in the area of propaganda—the ability to make black appear white and vice versa. His capacities in this direction were not surprising given his absolute contempt for the truth. He was, also, a totally cynical man—"man the beast" being one of his favorite phrases. He was born deformed, with an obvious limp. He was ugly inside and outside. A pig in clothes. He believed that his intelligence could overcome his ugly visage and his foul feet. Even his higher education, a Ph.D. from the University of Heidelberg, rarely led him to say anything resembling the product of wisdom. In the end, he stated with all his heart that he had come to hate the human race. His only act of courage was to order his own death before the fiery Russians could capture him.

Goebbels' opposite, a true believer with limited intelligence, was Rudolf Hess. As he often stated, he believed that Hitler was Germany, and his affection for the great leader was genuine. He would often speak before the Fuehrer and introduce him in the early days of the struggle for power. Before this, he helped with important party matters and displayed some organizational skill. Hitler admired him. Yet, being essentially naive, by 1941 Hess began to fall from favor among the more ruthless characters around him.

Later that year, he made a laughable solo flight to England in the mistaken belief that he could bring peace and spent the rest of the war in British captivity. In prison, he continued to believe in Hitler.

Finally, there was an odd assortment of lackeys, opportunists. and sycophants. Wilhelm Keitel and Alfred Jodl were despicable lackeys who displayed little independence from Hitler's ideas. Albert Speer, despite his intelligence, was an opportunist who used his friendship with Hitler to further his own career: as Chief Architect and later as the head of war production throughout the Reich. He was brought to justice at Nuremberg and sentenced to twenty years.

Reinhard Heydrich was a butcher: "Hangman" Heydrich, as he was called in the occupied lands. An able organizer, his career seemed fruitful until he was assassinated in June 1942. And finally there was Alfred Rosenberg, the so-called philosopher of Nazism, a stupid, dull fool. Hitler later appointed him to supervise the executions in Russia, and he paid for this with his life at Nuremberg. The late Alfred Rosenberg! I love that adjective: late.

These are the men who constituted the top leadership of the Third Reich. They and many others debased a nation that had given the world Goethe and Kant. Not only did these men hate each other, they also ran an incompetent and corrupt government full of intrigues, power struggles, and duplication of services or functions. This is one of the reasons why Germany lost the war. But, why did Hitler appoint these men? There are two possible reasons.

First, He could have chosen them because such men could never threaten his supreme position. This is certainly why he chose the late Alfred Rosenberg to head the party while he was in prison for treason after the Beer Hall Putsch. Under this dullard, the party would go nowhere, which is exactly where Hitler wanted it to go during that period.

The second reason is that our leader needed men like this to carry out his nefarious policies. Who else could be more suitable to carry out the New Order? Or, to put it another way, men like this were well adapted to the nature of his government. There was almost a symbiotic relationship here and the result was the rule of the lowest of the low. Of course, anyone who rose above this level of baseness was eliminated—as Gregor Strassser was—whose mistake was to believe truly in the socialist idea of Nazism. Plato, in his famous vision of society, wrote of men of gold, of silver, and of brass. These were men of dirt.

The lowest level of the soil included Adolf Hitler. What a strange and complex man! What sort of man dreams of utopia and then orders his followers to lie, cheat, steal, and even commit mass murder in order to achieve it? Certainly, no normal man. Hitler was the sort of double-minded man that Saint Paul spoke about thousands of years ago. On one level, he appeared normal. Yet, in other areas, he was quite insane. He loved to throw himself on the floor and chew on the edges of the carpet. Hence, he was referred to as a "carpet eater": *Teppichfresser!* In the "House of German Art" in Munich, he became so furious at some of the ideas expressed in these paintings that he threw several out the door and kicked holes with his jack boot through several others. He chose a notorious quack, Theodore Morell, to be his personal physician. Later, Morell would almost kill Hitler with poisonous injections. Also, Hitler had an obsession with blood—a lust for blood. He believed that historical greatness required the spilling of blood. The idea of a bloody death excited him, and this probably had some deep psychological significance. The Fuehrer was a completely abnormal man and, in the end, his insanity knew no limits and could not be stayed.

As for myself, I was fighting for my life among these madmen. Maybe, some external force would save me! It was possible that Germany could be defeated before the end of my trial, and this would lead to my liberation. This elated me only for a moment, however. Possible, but not likely. I might as well hope for the intervention of God. The situation was bad! The Americans and the British were approaching from France, and the Russians from Poland—that ridiculous state! How long could we hold them off? To Adolf Hitler—forever! Pure will could overcome anything in his eyes! Yet, all reasonable Germans knew the real answer—not long!

Whether this collapse would help me was another matter. I needed more than a short-term solution. But, what? The more I thought, the more I fell in despair.

The remedy, of course, was faith, and the nemesis of faith was reason. Ah, here was the problem. The belief in an all-good, all-powerful God would make every problem seem tolerable. As Nietzsche said, if man has a *why* in life, he could put up with any *is*. How true! My trouble was that I saw no meaning in any of the events occurring around me. If suffering helped me participate in the passion of Christ, then I could find meaning through ultimate transcendence. And how I needed this!

Yet, my mind could not assent. What is this faith in Christ, anyway? Christ was born two thousand years ago in a relatively obscure part of the Roman empire. The first thirty years of his life are to this day unknown, and the four gospels were written decades after his departure. During this time, most of mankind never heard of Christ. Great civilizations—the Chinese and the Egyptians—preceded him. Prehistory all the way back to Cro-Magnon man and beyond contains no record of his presence. Were these people not worthy of salvation? And is not his appearance in Judea somewhat arbitrary and preferential in favor of the peoples living there at that time? Why were peoples of different races in different historical eras excluded? To this day, large segments of mankind have no awareness of Jesus Christ.

The question of miracles is another matter. Skeptics, of course, deny these miracles ever occurred; many of them are not believable even on a simple commonsense level. For example, during the miracle known to Roman Catholics as the Ascension, Christ physically raises himself upward to the angels in heaven. But is this sensible? According to first-century cosmology, heaven, or the realm inhabited by God, was pictured as spatially above the earth while hell, or the realm of the damned, was in the underworld. Now, no one today can reasonably believe this. Above us is only space, including our own atmosphere, planets, and stars. Our sun is an ordinary star. Even if there is a heaven, it is not physically above us as hell is not below us. These were antiquated notions from a pre-scientific world view. Yet, in this story, Christ physically moves upward, indicating that the story is apocryphal. And, by the way, even if this and other miracles were true, what would it prove? It would only demonstrate that Christ possessed extraordinary powers, but it would not demonstrate his divinity. Other religious leaders from different traditions have performed miracles. Why not believe in their divinity? Even evil men, such as Rasputin, have had unusual powers. Am I to believe that he was the son of God?

Also, I had one other barrier to faith: I could not believe in an afterlife. Death is the end of all things, and it makes no sense to talk of a being that is born and never dies. Death is both a natural end and a desirable one. If there were a soul, it must be continuous throughout nature and exist everywhere, including within other animals. We Christians were taught, however, that only man has a soul. But, why? All organisms are made from the same protoplasm and go through a similar evolutionary development. Hindu and Shinto masters teach that animals are sacred in addition to man. This idea includes other primitive religions as well. (While hunting, the great Napoleon once observed that the stomach of a pig resembled the analogous human organ. A pig, he reasoned, digests like me. Hence, if I have a soul, so has he! And Napoleon was correct.)

But, even if man's soul existed, why should its activity during this ephemeral life be the basis of our future rewards or punishments in the next life? Or, to put it another way, if one is good for the duration of this life, why should one be given an eternal reward? Or, in the reverse circumstances, an eternal punishment? It really appears to be quite arbitrary and unjust. Evil or goodness for a short span should not receive an infinite sanction.

Yet, at another level, how I needed faith! I wish that I could have blinded my eye of reason in order to embrace the irrational truths of Christianity. One thing the Christian world view gave you was hope—the ability to go on one more day with conviction. I lacked that hope and could do no more than stare into the abyss of nothingness. In that void, I saw feces and urine. In my dreams, I saw worse: I was in a pit of dung or vomit, which was not far from the conditions throughout Germany and this prison.

The bombings continued. Germany was being made one vast wasteland. What made it worse for me was the knowledge that I would never be evacuated if the prison were hit directly. I would certainly die.

I could never come to terms with the notion of my death. Other people's deaths I could easily accept. But my death was inconceivable. I would not be in the world. I recoiled. Somehow, I had to survive despite the circumstances.

As the summer progressed into the fall, it seemed that my best chance was the military collapse of the Third Reich. Germany was being assaulted on all sides: our resistance in Italy had nearly collapsed, the Americans were approaching through Belgium, and the Russians were reconquering Poland. If Germany surrendered, I might be released unharmed. Time seemed to be on my side. Since the argument with Weissmann, I had not even been called for a consultation. My day of reckoning appeared to be far off. And there were more important undesirables than me to be eliminated. I now know, from the perspective of forty years, that the cynical men of the German General Staff were among these. I was glad for that! They were more than willing to cooperate with Hitler when he was rebuilding the armed forces. Hence, I danced when they died as a result of Hitler's wrath. Some were strangled by piano wire suspended from meat hooks! Without mercy! Rommel, too! Although it was not generally known in 1944, he was charged with high treason and given a choice of either committing suicide or standing trial before the dreaded People's Court. Since Judge Freisler's verdict would certainly have been guilty, Rommel chose suicide. I wouldn't shed a tear since Rommel was the general who gave our dear Leader all of those great conquests in Africa in 1942. Rommel lusted for glory, and glory's price was often death. At least, in the madhouse we called the Third Reich. As I say, I was glad these men died since their trials preoccupied the Nazi hierarchy in the People's Court—thus, granting me more time to survive. Existence is the first category. If you didn't exist, you were nothing. And I wanted to exist.

Of course, I was better off than the Jews. They received no trial at all. They simply were rounded up like wild dogs and massacred. This was an unprecedented historical tragedy. Was I partially responsible? Probably. I had been a loyal Nazi in my early days, even though I later became a pariah. I should have known the direction into which Hitler was leading the nation. (He had often told the masses that the symbol of all evil is the face of the Jew.) The holocaust did not occur overnight but, rather, was a gradual process that could have been prevented in time—if, that is, we had had the will to stop it. It began with anti-Semitism and a few beatings of local Jews.

Anti-Semitism had existed for thousands of years in Europe, and the Jews were the eternal outcasts. In my youth, many of my elders hated them and imparted that hatred to me. I was never a consummate anti-Semite, but I participated in the disease. A few Jews were beaten. What was my response? Good! I never stopped to consider that no Jew had ever harmed me or ever given me an unkind word. That was more than I could say for the Christians.

This process then accelerated when Jews were denied their rights under the so-called Nuremberg Laws of September 15, 1935. Jews were no longer citizens. Their property was then attacked—and worse. On November 9,

1938, one of the worst pogroms in the history of Germany was carried out by the state police. And we now know it was done with Hitler's approval. Hundreds of houses and thousands of shops and synagogues were set on fire. More than twenty thousand Jews were arrested, and thirty-five were killed. It was a night of hell throughout Germany. Goering, however, was annoyed at the low death count. He remarked to Heydrich, "I wish you had killed two hundred Jews instead of destroying so many valuables!" Yet, I am in no position to condemn anyone else. I remembered the destruction. I can still visualize the fires. I felt bad, but I did nothing, being so busy with my personal life. Apathy accelerated disaster.

After the war began, the Special Action Groups or Extermination Squads were formed. Their function was simply mass killing, and the army leaders knew it. This is why I later had no sympathy for this swine. There were four Special Action Groups on the Russian front entitled A, B, C, and D, respectively. Each one followed different armies into battle When a town or city was captured, these Special Action Groups would move in and begin systematically killing the civilian population. The Jews were the main target, but there were others, including gypsies and communists. Once the Jews were identified, they were usually ordered to march into an open field and forced to undress. They then had to kneel before an open ditch where each one was shot in the back of the head and thrown into the abyss. These killings occurred over and over again throughout the Russian campaign. Special Group D was responsible for the death of more than ninety thousand people. The only satisfaction we can have is that after the war most of the commanders of these Special Action Squads were hanged. Hatred is one thing, barbarism is another. And we must not become barbarians.

Then, in 1942, the inconceivable happened—extermination camps. Millions were murdered by gas. New words were added to the vocabulary of the twentieth century: Auschwitz, Treblinka, Belsec, Sibibor, and Riga. The victims were shipped to these camps from all over Europe—a ride that ended in hell. In addition, there were gruesome medical experiments carried out in these places; humans being treated as guinea pigs. Polish women were given gas gangrene wounds to test if they would survive. Jews were injected with jaundice for the same reason. There were freezing experiments and high-altitude tests. Poison bullets were shot at Russian prisoners of war. All this was done in the name of science. It would have been better attributed to sadism.

The German medical profession must bear some responsibility since respected doctors were directing these criminal activities. Physicians throughout the Reich knew what was happening and did nothing. I always hated doctors! There is something in the nature of a doctor that is callous. They believed they were gods and had the right to mandate life or death for others. I say kill them! On the day they die, they will learn that they are not gods—as an evil Roman ruler once did! It would be easy to ignore all of this and turn away in denial, but all of us were to some degree responsible.

However, all of this did not help me. The fact that some were worse off than you was no reason to be satisfied with your fate. I still had a major problem: I felt like a caged animal, and I had nowhere to turn.

In December, my hopes for a quick end of the war seemed to end with the announcement of a great German offensive in Belgium. Our forces were apparently winning great victories against the Allied armies. Only later, did I learn that these reports were greatly exaggerated. In fact, this offensive doomed the German army since it depleted its reserves. The Fuehrer had been warned that the Russians would soon be attacking from Poland and that massive reserves would be needed there to support them. Now, those needed troops were either killed or captured. But, back then I did not know this and was plunged again into despair.

The best remedy for that was sleep, and I slept often. Yet, again my dreams were disturbing. I always seemed to go back to the houses on the street in London where I was born. Someone else was always falling, and I could not prevent it. I would, however, feel guilty about it and always hide. The houses were hideous, yet real. I always felt uncomfortable and could never escape from those searching for me. Eventually I would awake from my sleep. ("Perchance to dream," as the saying goes.) Yes, indeed! How I hated sleep and its intimation of death.

I had to think of something good. But, what? Women? What a record of failure. Few erections, too! Friends? I had none! Adolf Hitler? Yes, I had some fond recollections of him.

When I first came to Munich after the death of my parents, I was searching for a new life. And I had always been fascinated with German history. Hitler, in large part, provided me with new meaning and enthusiasm. Also, pride—a good feeling.

I remember specifically April 20, 1939, which was Hitler's fiftieth birthday. The center of Berlin was transformed into a huge military district where Hitler, seated on what appeared to be a golden throne, reviewed the armies of the Third Reich. Bright and erect, a modern Caesar Augustus, he repeatedly gave his soldiers the Nazi salute, an ancient Roman innovation. And they often reciprocated. It was an awesome sight. The leader and his cohorts in a grand unity. One could be proud to be a German.

I recall that day quite well; I was merely one of the nameless, faceless people on the streets of Berlin. There was a feeling of general well-being. German armed strength symbolized a slap in the face for England or France and the hated Versailles Treaty, which had tried to disarm the German nation. Now, we were strong again because of Adolf Hitler. (Even that name is a symbol!) It was truly a triumph of the will, and we all shared in the pride.

Also, a few days later another great event occurred. Franklin Roosevelt, the American president, sent our Fuehrer a telegram asking for a pledge that we would not attack or invade the nations of Europe. In front of the Reichstag on April 28, 1939, Hitler delivered a masterful reply. He heaped endless criticism on the American president—well deserved, in my modest judgement—and unveiled America's own disgraceful past. He reminded Roosevelt of the atrocities committed both against the Sioux tribes and the Africans. He also noted several historical errors in Roosevelt's letter. Ireland, for instance. The so-called president had the nerve to ask for a pledge that Germany would not attack Ireland. That land, Hitler pointed out, was subject to English, not German aggression. And the same was true of Palestine. Hitler then read and intoned the names of every country listed in the telegram as the laughter of the deputies in the Reichstag grew louder. He then assured America's leader that Germany had no intention of attacking the United States. How ridiculous! What a stupid telegram! As if a verbal guarantee would mean anything anyway! There was no greater time in my life.

Oh, the "good life" under Hitler. It was real. The economy was booming, and the nation was again a respected world power. For the common man, it felt good to be a German. The reasons why the economy was booming were quite apparent, although not noticed by most Germans. The main one was rearmament: the building blocks of the economy and war. Germany was a vast war machine with planes, tanks, and guns being manufactured daily. That war machine brought work to millions, but it would shortly kill millions. The average person, however, did not care. He was absorbed in his own private life or private dreams and the parades or charades of the Third Reich. Private dreams! These are dreams to fear—selfish desires that exclude the vast majority of mankind. America was the home of private dreams, with each man hoping to achieve his own utopia at the exclusion of all else. Now, Germany went through this stage of hedonism—a land of all against all. As in America, Germany became a land of the greedy, by the greedy, and for the greedy. May they both perish from the earth!

The early success of Hitler in foreign policy was due more to Hitler's opponents' weaknesses than to his own inner strength. France had lost more than one and a third million men during the Great War, not counting the wounded and missing. Her leaders resolved that there should never be another war. And England, too, had been mauled in a similar manner. The consequence, in large part, of the policy of appeasement, which gave Hitler so many bloodless victories, including the surrender at Munich on September 30, 1938. If the Fuehrer had wisdom, he would have stopped his aggression at this point and consolidated his gains. Yet, this man who desired to control Europe could not control himself. Hence, the attack on Poland on September 1, 1939 that would start a second world war—one of even greater destructive forces than the first. The British and the French leaders had by now seen through Hitler—too late as it turned out.

Our great leader had, of course, conquered an enormous empire by 1942. But this empire could not be held. Germany lacked the manpower and resources to maintain it. Moreover, a defeated people could not be controlled by force alone. The task required the resocialization of the unhappy people and the institutionalization of the Nazi doctrine, a process that needed considerable time. This time could not be found with a leader who continuously added one nation after another to our list of enemies. Any vanquished nation is more easily controlled from within than from without. But war was Hitler's method, and the doom of his empire was predetermined by it.

In the end, the illusion of the "good life" under Hitler was essentially a creation of Dr. Goebbels' propaganda machine. The reality was that Germany was being led my a mad, lazy, and incompetent leader who was leading the nation toward war. (Yes, Hitler was lazy; the day-to-day administration of the country bored him. He left this work to his associates, who carved up separate empires: Goering controlled the air force and the economy, Himmler controlled the Gestapo, Goebbels the Propaganda Ministry, and so on. This resulted in great confusion and inefficiency. Hitler concentrated on the war or the murder of the Jews, and given our limited resources, both could not be achieved.) Life may be based on illusions, but reality finally confronted the German people by early 1945.

Yet, the illusion of the "good life" was widely believed in the summer of 1939. I believed it myself. As I say, Germany was again the center of the civilized world. Every word, every gesture, and every action of Hitler was the news of the day. And this is why that swine Roosevelt hated him: envy, pure and simple! England and France were afraid of war, and our country was respected again. It was a beautiful summer; parades and festivals were everywhere. I did quite a bit of traveling, having both the money and leisure. True, there was talk of a possible war with Poland, but no one took that seriously. We assumed Hitler would negociate a peaceful settlement as in the cases of Austria and Czechoslovakia. To be blunt, we enjoyed the "good life" and were willing to forget about tomorrow.

But, of course, all that had now turned to ashes. Again, I had to think of something good! Were there other affirmations to which I could aspire? Were there other values that might again give me the will to live? I thought of the entire range of my life and could affirm nothing. Wait! There was one positive memory: my dog Kush. A sound and noble creature. One of intelligence and loyalty. A canine of speed and keen vision. To this day, I can only smile when I recall his comradeship. (Kush, I often nod gently to myself when speaking of him.) Yes, one of nature's more pitiable creatures. I loved him. And I mean true love, not the role-playing affection that often passes for the emotion. Rather, a genuine, selfless feeling—a love of what he had been and, in the end, had become: an invalid dog barely capable of walking. Nonetheless, although lame and often in pain, he was handsome. He had a deep, intrinsic nobility behind his shattered eyes. and his affections were genuine, which is more than I can say for the vast majority of the "sick species." Yet, even in his case, life was vile. To this day, his death remains a horrid memory.

Returning home late one cold November evening, I immediately sensed his dreadful fate. No noise from his quarter, not a stir. I found him on the floor. still and rigid. Horrible! I could neither grasp nor deal with the situation immediately; I simply lay in bed, incapacitated by troubled thoughts and totally unable to sleep. I felt nothing for some time—sometimes the point of a blade leaves you numb. But, as dawn approached, I had to act. Looking at him for the final time, I sobbed uncontrollably. In some respects, the grief was worse than it had been for my father. Kush seemed serene and at peace, as if relieved of a great burden. I then slowly wrapped him in an ordinary plaid sheet and carried him to his place of burial. Using a worn and rusted shovel, I began to dig. It may have been the most difficult thing I have ever done.

Digging, digging, and again digging deeper and deeper into the earth as his body laid adjacent to me under that mat. The pebbles grew larger, so it seemed, as I reached a depth of four or five feet. What a miserable ending: to be placed near large pebbles in the dirt. I continued to dig and dig again as allusions of Hamlet and Yorick passed through my mind. I stopped at seven feet and then tenderly placed him in that hole. "God bless you," I said repeatedly as I sobbed. I quickly covered him with the unclean soil and broke down. The world did not care for Kush, but I did. I prayed to the Supreme Father to bless Kush and to thank me for my concern. I read from my favorite Psalm. Perhaps sacred words would somehow sanctify his all too mundane life. The salvation of Christ normally does not extend to brutes, but I could not accept this. I cried out to God to open wide the gates to the land of Canaan so Kush could scurry untamed through that pure and noble canopy. Maybe, the Lord would hear the cry of one who loved him. Kush was a sentient, caring being devoid of sin. Indeed, in his presence, there were intimations of saintliness.

Miserable, isn't it? And I am not thinking only of his end but also of my reference. During my entire life, the only good thing I could recall was a dog.

CHAPTER SEVEN

The last days of the Apocalypse were upon me. I didn't know which was worse: man or his machine—man, an ignoble being, or man's machine-modern bureaucracy. Modern life was machine life, and the machine was not good. It allowed one to hide behind the task, often a diabolical task. The Third Reich was the ultimate outcome of the machine mentality. Input, output, production, efficiency. Specified tasks and central organization. It was no accident that Hitler embraced capitalism, with its greedy owners and exploited workers. The modern mass media provided the tools. Central control meant uniform ideas and one-dimensional man. Men were workers, women homemakers. Women's tasks were in the kitchen and the bedroom. Men were expected to be soldiers when needed. The routines of bureaucracy—specialization, hierarchy, regulations, and technical qualifications—provided the training for all of this. The ultimate machine state. The technicians were included as well as the scientists. They ran the ignoble apparatus. They were scum—machine scum. How I hated them! I hated their bald heads, their phony smiles and their smell. A knife through the heart, that's what they needed!

In late December, I was escorted from my cell to the Great Hall of Justice. You know, human justice must be the work of an inferior god, one of limited intelligence. I was rudely seated at the counsel's table next to the odious Dr. Weissmann. He did not attempt so much as a gesture toward me. As a practitioner of the absurd, he would have been better known in the absence. I then glanced forward, and a demonic figure gradually emerged. Although partially engulfed in shadows, he slowly began to take form as a glimmering of light filled the vacuum. It was Judge Roland Freisler, the President and Chief Magristrate of the People's Court. Three huge and colorful swastikas decorated the wall behind him. He, himself, wore a black robe and hat. My impressions were immediately morbid: an expressionless face, deep piercing eyes, and a shrieking, almost hysterical voice. He seemed devoid of any humanity. His greeting had a subterranean odor: "Bertrand Sovare, rise now!" I rose, and he then proceeded to ask me a few perfunctory questions. "Are you a Professor at the University of Munich?"

"Yes," I responded curtly.

He continued: "You have taught the odious work of the Jews, Freud, and Einstein. Have you not?"

I kept calm while attempting to answer. "Your Excellency, I would like to explain."

He then demanded hysterically, "Simply answer yes or no!"

"Yes," I said with resignation.

"Yes," he shrieked as he began to intone every word, "you are a worthless bum devoid of all self-respect. You think you can decide what is right apart from our Fuehrer, the leader of us all!" I tried to continue. He interrupted: "You dirty dog. Stop playing with your trousers!" Actually, this was no fault of mine since the pants I was given were oversized, and I had no belt. I had to hold up my trousers. That, of course, meant nothing to this magistrate.

I continued without emotion. "I taught what I believed from conscience."

"Conscience," he screamed, "you are a despicable creature. Despicable! Your punishment was preordained and now ordered." He then handed a court official a document while he continued ranting and screaming. Hell itself could not have been worse. Weissmann still remained silent; not a word came forward in my defense.

My punishment was preordained and, no doubt, would normally have been rendered immediately: death by hanging. I was quite shaken when I was escorted back to my cell. I felt as if I was here and yet not here; I could not believe that this was really happening. I looked at the whole of my life as I anticipated its end. And what a tragic record of misery that was. I simply sat alone with my thoughts and waited.

But, surprisingly, nothing happened! I could not understand why. I certainly could not have received mercy from a maniac like Freisler. I continued to wonder, but no answer came. As I looked at my death, I realized how short life was. And how great a failure I was: not one of the great ideals of my youth had been achieved. A life well spent leads to an easy sleep; a life of failure leads to a miserable death . My death was different from other people's deaths. Death was all around me, yet it did not affect me. But my death was the end of my world, a confrontation with nothingness. I simply would disappear. I always had trouble accepting death; I could never accept my parents' deaths. I even pretended to others that Kush was alive long after his demise. (As if when I referred to him in the present, he might still be around somewhere.) And my death, above all, repelled me. I determined that I must survive. I must survive! If I died, I must take my own life.

That wish almost became unnecessary due to the unending air attacks on Berlin. Certainly I would die in one, and then nothing else would matter. I hoped my body would be cremated; I hated cemeteries. I didn't want anyone to say that I was there. I, also, hated the inequality of those places. Some died young, others full of years. Some were content before death, others miserable. Some had huge monuments, others inconsequential ones. Even in death, nothing was fair here. (How I hated this "sick species"!) I never visited my parents grave after their demise; I could never look at their names on a tombstone. You see, my father's name was also Bertrand Sovare. I guess it was my way of negating death.

It was January 1, 1945. A short distance from my cell there were four SS guards with a radio. They turned it on so they could listen to Hitler's message commemorating the new year. I listened, too, and knew immediately that something was amiss. Hitler almost never spoke in public anymore. I had heard him on the radio only twice in the past two years. (This was quite different from the earlier days of the struggle. His voice would then be heard hundreds of times.) At first, I thought he might announce our surrender, but his first words gave a different impression: defiance! He was a piece of steel. We would fight to the end! We would never surrender! Never! He assured us that we had been through greater difficulties before and had mastered them. We would soon smash our enemies! New miracle weapons would deliver the barbarian Russians a Stalingrad. We would then crush the Americans completely. And the English would, no doubt, lay down their arms. He ended with an appeal to us to place faith in him and our great destiny. Even in prison, my passions were moved by the speech. Yet, my feelings were confused. Hitler had not lost his gift for oratory. He could convince you hat black was white. I knew that Germany's defeat was in my interest, but I still hoped that we could stop the Russians. There was something about Hitler that made you live again, some great charisma that was the basis of his power. And I assume the same was true of his influence on other people. The Germans would now fight to the bitter end.

One of the Fuehrer's greatest appeals was that he was nonintellectual. He had intellect but spoke to something deeper than the intellect: the will to power and the irrational instincts of man. He knew of the passionate contradictions in our being. He knew what a vile creature man was. (And woman, too! Women, actually, were the most ardent fascists. They loved Hitler. Women love criminals, and Hitler was the greatest criminal of all time.) Somehow, you believed Hitler when he spoke because you sensed that he believed in what he said. And that is more than you can say for most intellectuals! As a thinker, I still despised them: *intellectuals love books, not people*. They speak *down* and not *to* other men. Their realm of ideas is not in the sphere of our world. (This is why we burned all those books. And I engaged in it. Books could never capture the ecstasy of Adolf Hitler.) He spoke of ordinary and simple things—common dreams that we might all achieve together. And when we failed, it was like a falling-out among American gangsters.

I hoped intellectuals would be relegated to the trash can of history. Their way was not our way. I was an anti-intellectual thinker: the intellect must serve our instincts. And, above all, the interests of the state. It must not be a free-floating intellect without an anchor, aimless and disparate. Most thinkers are socially unattached individuals; therein lies their uselessness. By deliberate choice, they have no power base to carry out their ideas. And what good are ideas without power? In this respect, I have never known a more absurd suggestion than Plato's idea that philosophers should rule the state. I know that he was speaking of an ideal state, but, in reality, philosophers are useless—they are not taken seriously, they are isolated, and their ideas have little relevance to the world. But, even if they had power, they would not retain it for long. Genius in philosophy and political ability are entirely disparate. Imagine a philosopher concerned with the ontological argument trying to maintain the allegiance of the German army. Laughable! (And this argument for God's existence was taken seriously by some thinkers at the university. In short, if God is defined as the most perfect being, then he must exist since existence is a perfection. The argument also has other forms. Kant rejected it.) I was glad that I had few comrades at the University of Munich.

Now, however, I would greet any comrade. In an adjacent cell, I could see a former officer named Fromm; I can't remember his first name. Occasionally, we exchanged a few words. He had been sentenced to death, and I asked him if Freisler sentenced him immediately. He answered that he had learned of his fate two weeks after his court appearance. I then wondered why he had not already been hanged. Perhaps I too would be given more time before facing the king of terrors. And then suddenly he was no longer there. He disappeared. Later, I learned that he had been shot by a firing squad.

In a way, the end was approaching faster than anyone had thought possible. On January 12, 1945, the great Russian offensive in Poland began with such ferocity that within two weeks the Reds were only one hundred miles from Berlin. Panic spread everywhere; SS guards spoke openly within the prison's corridors of the impending disaster. Imagine! The barbarians were about to capture the capital of the Third Reich. Unthinkable a few years earlier! We controlled almost all of Europe, and our army was the most powerful in the world. How did we fall into this state? It seems to me today that the fall of Nazism began with the very nature of the Nazi philosophy itself: it was not a life-giving or a life-generating belief system. There was something essentially nihilistic about Nazism—a basic hatred of life on this planet. Germanic greatness and empire were mere rationalizations. The essence of Nazism was simply the urge for destruction, and this was the ultimate reason for every step in this direction. Each step appeared to be independent, but, in reality, there was a pattern.

First, the very idea of a world war in 1939 was irrational. Germany was not prepared for such a war. This was especially true in regard to our naval production; our lack of natural resources ensured disaster. In the beginning, the nation was protected by the Nazi-Soviet Pact, which allowed us to fight alone on the western front. But after the attack on Russia on June 22, 1941, and the later Allied invasions on Italy and Normandy, Germany had to fight on three fronts. This was simply too much for our armies. (And Italy was a worthless partner. The Italians simply ran away in battle. They were a disgrace!) Even so, if the German generals had the freedom to conduct their campaigns according to their knowledge of military science, then all might have been well. Hitler, however, constantly interfered with all sorts of untested and irrational ideas that accelerated defeat.

Thus, the course of the war was determined not by proper strategy, but by Hitler's singular psychology. By the way, there was no economic or political reason for war in 1939 except the urge for war in our insane leader's mind. Nor was there any pressing need to attack Russia in 1941. In fact, it might have been the worst thing to do at that time since England was not defeated. The invasion was a result of a desire in Hitler's mind—going back to 1925—to crush Russia. It was expressed in an early slogan from that period: "Adolf Hitler devours Karl Marx"! The attack made no sense in another manner: it did not concentrate on a few limited objectives. Rather, the German army attacked on a broad front from the Baltic to the Black Sea. The front had little inner depth at any point, and the objectives were too diffuse. In the end, this resulted in disaster when the Russians began to counterattack. Above all, Hitler's decision to declare war on the United States on December 11, 1941, was his greatest blunder. Once again, he did not have to declare war since his pact with Japan mandated that he do this only if Japan was herself attacked by another power. But, it was Japan who attacked Pearl Harbor on the day of infamy. The real reason was the Fuehrer's irrational hatred of America and Americans. The fact that America was the world's greatest industrial power seems not to have troubled him. This decision doomed the Third Reich. And it also demonstrated that Hitler was a phony. The Japanese were by his own racial theory an inferior race.

As if this was not enough, Hitler decided after 1941 to fight another war: the war against the Jews. Of course, there was mass murder committed against the Jews before this time, but never with the intensity that followed. Now there were extermination camps—and they were not simply concentration camps. Auschwitz became the most famous. All Jews were to be killed throughout Europe. Yet, this was an entirely emotional decision that was devoid of logic and common sense. The Jews were not Germany's enemy. And, morals aside, the decision to destroy them tied up human and material resources needed for the war effort. This was especially true in regard to transportation facilities that were used to carry the Jews or others to Auschwitz or similar camps. Germany's defeat, in this respect, was poetic justice. This was a result of Hitler's decision since no major policy was carried out without his approval.

Also, as I said before, the entire Nazi revolution occurred too quickly and was not given the time to be incorporated into the German tradition. New folkways, mores, and laws need decades, if not centuries, to mix properly into an overall culture. Yet, Hitler tried to carry out his revolution in only a few years. He spoke constantly of a "Thousand Year Reich," but he did not really mean it. He did not want anyone else to finish his work; he believed he had to do it all himself. An evil god cannot conceive of another deity finishing his creation. In the end, he did not wish that anyone else would benefit from his life work. That is why he left nothing except destruction.

This evil god, in addition, did not take advantage of major opportunities. The most important came before the invasion of Russia. He should have attacked the British through Egypt, which almost certainly would have resulted in their defeat. Even during the Russian campaign, he refused to be flexible and give the generals autonomy. And his lack of concern for the German atomic bomb project doomed it to failure. In the end, Field Marshal von Brauchitsch was right. He said, "Hitler was the fate of Germany, and that fate could not be stayed." The fall of the Third Reich was due to Adolf Hitler—his personal limitations, his mental illness, and his monstrous evil. He wanted to conquer the world, but he could not conquer himself. The words of a despised king could easily apply to him: "What do I fear? Myself? There's none else by. Richard loves Richard: that is, I am I."

His end, however, involved us all. As for myself, I would rather die here than fall into Russian hands, to be sent to the Liublanka and be devoured by rats. I hated rats! I could see my corpse being eaten by them. What a fate! No doubt, Hitler was one of the greatest failures in history. I sometimes wonder whether he really wanted to win. Or to put it another way, it seems almost as if he was aiming at destruction. He said, "If the war is lost, the nation will also perish. This fate is inevitable." Germany must be destroyed and also the world, if possible. It must be a world in ruins. Unknown to me at the time, Hitler had issued his famous "Nero Order" on March 19, 1945. All military, transportation, business, and residential, areas were to be blown up to prevent them from falling into the hands of the enemy. Nothing was to be left for future generations of Germans. This was the ultimate solipsism: if Hitler went out of existence, then so must Germany. By the way, this was a serious order and would have been carried out if it were not for the rapid movement of the Allied armies. Also, if Germany had the atomic bomb, our dear leader undoubtedly would have used it, and unbelievable destruction would have ensued. Hitler might have destroyed the earth. He certainly destroyed the German army.

He insisted that no German soldier be allowed to retreat a single step no matter how desperate or useless continued resistance was. This led to the massacre of large segments of the German army. Hundreds of thousands of men were decimated in hopeless or encircled positions. No enemy could have inflicted more damage on us than our dear leader did. Commanders who disobeyed orders were shot, and their families were executed. Even the defense of Berlin was being conducted in a suicidal manner: young men were sacrificed for no reason at all while the Russians occupied the city house by house. In this way, Hitler's life would be saved for a few days.

Sigmund Freud died in London in 1939. If he had lived a few more years, he would have seen the greatest historical confirmation of his ideas on the death instinct in man. Yes, in the deep recesses of the mind, the urge for self-preservation breaks down. The unconscious mind desires incest, self-mutilation, blood, feces, and death. There we want to return to the original state of nonbeing from which we came. This logic is as powerful as Aristotle's—and more potent in determining everyday affairs. Hitler's life and Hitler's Reich proved that every man and every group of men have within themselves the seeds of their own destruction—that man does not aim toward utilitarian or pragmatic purposes but, rather, toward death and desolation. After me the deluge! And the Third Reich was the realization of this unconscious fantasy.

In the interval between these thoughts, the Prussian Junkers were being decimated. I was not one of them. And I hoped that I could avoid their fate. Again, I tried to think of something good and often thought back to my university days. At that time, after my lectures, I would return to my study. Under a portrait of Johann Gottlieb Fichte, I would sit in my armchair and study his philosophy. What a transcendent experience! I realize now that we never appreciate the good times until after they are gone. And how I needed good times now!

My situation became so desperate that I longed for human companionship. How ironical that I should need other people. Yet, I did. And one of the most important people that I knew during this period was Fabian von Schlabrendorff. I spoke to him intermittently since he occupied one of the adjacent cells. I could think of few people that I have ever known whom I admired so much as he. Fabian was one of the very few and earliest conspirators against Hitler. Above all, he was a man of high idealism. He opposed Hitler on moral grounds and was willing to put his life on the line. He was never seduced by our dear leader. He had participated in several critical attempts to kill Hitler long before the July 20, 1944 plot.

One of the most interesting occurred in 1943. A bomb was smuggled onto the leader's plane, and it was expected to explode in midair. It never did and the plane landed safely; the bomb proved to be defective. Later, there were several so-called overcoat attempts . Several courageous volunteers were wired with bombs under their overcoats and agreed to blow both Hitler and themselves up at the earliest opportunity. Yet, due to various factors, these attempts were never finalized. And, of course, Stauffenberg's plan misfired. Now, as with all the other conspirators, Schlabrendorff was on trial for his life. He was a realist. He knew that he had to die and accepted it. I admired this. The only true freedom man has is the ability to give or take his own life. To be manipulated in death is agony; to die freely is the highest station of man.

I thought of this idea often. You know, the real reason for my failure in life lies in my uncontrolled fear of death. How often I have not lived life to the fullest because of this basic fear. Julius Caesar said it best in a famous play: "Cowards die many times before their deaths; the valiant never taste of death but once." I regard this as a great existential truth. My fear of death and my denial of death have led me to this state. A coward I have lived, and so a coward I must die. I now know that to overcome the fear of death is the first step toward living as a moral being. My moral baseness is directly related to my physical cowardice. I am unwilling to die, which renders me unable to live. Fear prevented me from true love and conviction. Fear allowed me to be manipulated and controlled by the evil one.

Fear has led me to be a slave to my emotions and base instincts. Great men do not fear death. Saint Paul had no fear. "To live is Christ and to die is gain," he often said. He was willing to die at any moment to live the word of Christ. Socrates did not fear death, and this bold attitude made him one of the world's greatest philosophers. He would die for his convictions. To be able to die for one's beliefs is the most noble deed in this bemired world. All great men have mastered their fear of death. If you do not conquer your fear of death, that fear will conquer you. And I have surrendered.

Now there are many types of courage: physical, moral, and intellectual. I clearly do not have physical courage. My main emotion is fear—uncontrolled fear. I also am what Nietzsche called a moral monster. Devoid of feeling toward others, I am an objectification of greed. I do, however, have intellectual courage. I have studied the great works of man with one essential aim: to find the truth. What is truth? I am as confused today as on the day I began my inquiry. No! Truth is being able to live and not just to think. Life is meant to be enjoyed and not simply thought about. In my days, I have done too much thinking and too little living. You know, John Dewey was right: thought and action must be combined in any true educational experience. A liberal arts education—what good is it? To live an aimless life of contemplation without conviction, without anchor, and without emotional balance. A great education must promote all three types of courage. The first two are the most important ones; the third is an appendix. My life is an appendix, a vestigial organ on the body of humanity.

As a diversion from these grand thoughts, I often switched to smaller ones. The small things made a difference. Occasionally I would be given a hot beverage, which I savored. I let my mind go blank and enjoyed the moment. And this renewed me, no doubt, for additional episodes of pain. So much of life consisted of small pleasures: a modest meal, a cup of soup, or an agreeable face (Ha, there were no agreeable faces!) It reminded me of the famous old remark: we live in order to eat and eat in order to live. It seemed so purposeless and endless. Life lives on other life; this is the great truth of all ancient religions and philosophies. We live to eat on the flesh of other beings, both animal and vegetable. Yet, I could not accept it; I could not accept mere existence as the end of all striving. There must be something more. There must be something that makes it all worth while. The Christ should have provided that, but I chose Adolf Hitler. Adolf Hitler was my god. To look at him was to look at the face of the deity. His doctrine of redemption was one: the higher man. This man would be a military being of great physical perfection. His mind would exhibit the highest virtues of courage, loyalty, and craftiness. He would be immune from the petty weaknesses of bourgeois man. Above all, he would constitute a new species qualitatively superior to the human race. Yes, that's what the Fuehrer would provide: a new creation—a second genesis! A chance to improve mankind and provide a great new Reich in all its glory, strength, righteousness, and justice. Amen! It was a religion. Yes, and yes again, my god was Adolf Hitler! I sought glory so mighty that I forgot about humanity. I looked so high that I did not see what was near. I felt that every means justified my illicit ends. I wanted to be a god and in the process became a beast. I became anything but human.

Nazism was a doctrine of final ends, an apocalyptic vision. And if heaven could not be obtained, then hell was at hand. If the higher man could not be perfected, than man himself must be destroyed. Yes, better to reign in hell than serve in heaven, as someone once said. (I think it was Satan, but who gives a damn.) As Satan, Hitler was now the high demonic priest. After the war, I learned of his orders, which I have already discussed. Scorched earth and total destruction! Again, all of Germany was to be blown up—all electrical and industrial plants, gas and water facilities, clothing and food stores, communication and railway installations, and all ships, bridges, and locomotives. Nothing would be left; we would all be sacrificed at the altar of our would-be messiah. A new Last Judgement. Yes, the verdict of an evil god: the German people are unworthy of me, and they must perish. Is this really any different from the Christian Last Judgement? There a so-called benevolent God sentences most of mankind to hell for sins committed during our typical three score and ten—or less as in the case of whores. How irrational! (Why must we be judged anyway? It's almost as if we're constantly being tested and for what reason no one knows. Why can't we live for the moment and in peace?) In any case, our dear leader's doctrine of final ends required a creative mythology and a final judgment. Above all, for the Fuehrer himself. Thus, if his end were glorious enough, he might live on in legend—a legend that could inspire the rebirth of Nazism. And in this he succeeded: *Adolf Hitler is alive*! You're never really dead as long as people talk about you—as long as you inspire others to noble deeds. And this is what he is still doing. People are fascinated with him, his movement, and the war. It goes on to this day! The only true heaven is mythology. (The other heaven is for nuns, impotent old fools, and English whores.) And Hitler has more influence in the realm of mythology than most people do who are living at this moment.

But, in my prison, at least, there were some of us who did not want to burn at the funeral pyre. A dead hero of Greek mythology prayed to be put back on the earth; he would rather be a serf in the house of some landless man than king of all the dead ones that were done with life. And I, too, would rather have been a serf. The underworld is not better than the air; the good earth does have its delights. Yet, I realize that I was wrong: that was the right time to die. As Hitler said, "It's just one brief moment and you're free of everything. Just everlasting peace and tranquility." Yet, for some reason, I did not want this. As I said—it was fear pure and simple. Some men live too long. I certainly am one of them. Others were not so lucky. The dreaded People's Court was still in session and Freisler was grinding out death sentences daily. But, not for long. On February 3,

1945, as Schlabrendorff was being led into the courtroom, an American bomb fell directly on the courthouse killing Freisler and resulting in the freedom of a wide group of conspirators who escaped in the confusion. Fabian was not one of them, yet he had been spared a certain death by hanging. He was jubilant and later said to me, "You see, it is the hand of God. Freisler was the judge, and now he is dead. I was to be judged, and I am alive." I thought of that for a time. Freisler was a pig, and his death was quite appropriate. It almost seemed to be a divine judgement. Could this be possible? I later learned that Freisler had already left the courthouse for the air raid shelter when he recalled that he left papers on his desk. He went back—to die! Did the true God make him return? He could easily have taken the papers with him. But, when he returned, his skull was fractured. And today he rests in an unmarked grave. Yes, it could have been the hand of our Creator. I thought back to the teaching of my former Christian friends: the true God had given us a way of life and a path of destruction. The Ten Commandments promise a way of life or salvation, and disobedience to these divine rules provides the other path, the one modern man has taken. Perhaps this is why Freisler died and Germany was being blown apart. And, I must say, why I am going to perdition. We don't worship the true God. In Leviticus 26, God promises peace and abundance to those who obey his statuses. God offers freedom from fear: "And ye shall chase your enemies, and they shall fall before you by the sword." But, to those who hate God and his commandments, God pronounces death and worse. "I will appoint over you terror, consumption, and the burning ague, that shall consume the eyes and cause sorrow of heart." The true God continues, "I will set my face against you, and ye shall be slain before your enemies. They that hate you shall reign over you, and ye shall flee when none pursueth you." This is, as I think of it, the story of my entire life: terror, fear, and being ruled over by enemies. It is also the story of our nation. By making Adolf Hitler god, we mocked the true Creator and thus brought destruction on our own house.

You know, it is impossible to live in fear if you really believe in the promises of the true God. If you really believe that God created the heavens and the earth, then you cannot live in fear. Fear is an absence of faith. Faith in Christ! To live in Christ is to know that God can cure your diseases, bring you happiness, give you mental peace, and overcome your fear before death. I, Bertrand Sovare, rejected the true God. I sought a substitute: glory, knowledge, abnormal sex, money, and Hitler. And I am reduced to nothing.

Nothing! The fault lies not in the nature of things but in myself. I wanted to rule my own life. I could not bow before the true one. If only I could go back through time and pay God respect. How great I could have been! How much love I could have received! Through others, as directed by God, I would have been led to the path of laughter and abundance. The joy of children, of grandchildren, and of brothers and sisters in Christ. Fear could not have controlled me, but I would have conquered fear. The heaven above would have been the heaven below. Oh, time reverse yourself! Stop now and go back so that these memories may fade away and become nothing in my sight! The joy of the true God I still can reach but I dare not touch.

Yet, once again, my will remained supreme, and I ignored this truth. I was not convinced. There were too many contrary instances, too many other cases where evil was triumphant. In Freisler's situation, things came out the right way. But, this simply could have been the work of chance. An arbitrary chance. That's one thing that I can't tolerate about religion: its inherent unfairness. Christ cured one cripple who came his way but left all the others in the world in misery. It does appear a bit preferential, to say the least. If God intervenes in the affairs of the world, he should do so universally and without exception, not just in isolated cases. Unless, that is, his kingdom is the "kingdom of the arbitrary." What heavenly plan could kill Freisler and leave so many equally dreadful people unscathed? It was all too irrational for me to accept.

As always, Schopenhauer was illuminating: the world itself is the ultimate judge of the world. Because our inner nature is evil, we produce a world that is selfish and base—and which in its turn moves back to condemn us. We do not deserve to be happy, and so we are miserable. In fact, we do not deserve to exist, and so we cease to exist. The nature of this vile world is our ultimate condemnation. And so it was with the Third Reich. Our movement, after all, saw the rise of the lowest element in Germany: murderers, rowdies, drug addicts, sexual perverts, pimps, blackmailers, sadists, and anti-Semites. This scum ruled the Fatherland, and we have only ourselves to blame for the catastrophe. We intellectuals deserve the largest share of the blame, and I do not exclude myself. I have called Kozik a coward. But, so am I. We were too interested in ideas to be concerned with injustice. We did not realize that ideas should be the servant of the world—not a tool merely to interpret it. And so I am not facing death without some justice—in the sense that I helped my accusers to attain power. Yes! The world itself is the judge of the world.

And the world seemed increasingly Red! Those communists were a mere one hundred miles from Berlin, and their artillery bombardment was merciless. Five thousand big guns! Explosions were everywhere! Hitler was back in Berlin, which he had barely seen since the beginning of the war. Apparently, we would defend the city to the last man and the last round. Madness! The war was lost! In the west, the Americans had crossed the Rhine, the last natural barrier in that area. Remagen bridge had been left intact by our forces, and enemy units quickly raced across it. Hitler had eight German commanders there executed for this mishap. And I agreed with his decision. There is an old saying: stupidity has never helped anybody yet. Now, we were at the mercy of the enemy, and our country lay in ruins. This killed me! The most annoying thing was that England always escaped unscathed, her territory intact. That nation always fought and devastated the land and peoples of other countries. Dr. Goebbels said it right: "God punish England!" And I wished that somehow, even at this late stage of history, she would be punished. (Ha! As fate would have it, later I did enjoy watching her empire collapse. Yes! I savored watching her being reduced to little England! As Napoleon once said, "With God's help, I will destroy the destiny and the very existence of England." Too bad he failed in this ambition; we would all be better off.) And, again, we should have finished off England before attacking Russia. I will never understand why we did not. Perhaps, Hitler thought that Russia would collapse quickly. They did in the Great War. Now, however, they were ruled by Stalin, a despot who almost equaled Hitler. And the Soviet armies were stronger and better directed than in 1917. In any case, our attack on this horrible nation in 1941 sealed our fate!

The Reds were encircling Berlin. The artillery fire was constant; the smoke was everywhere. From the distance of the prison, I could see the fires. The SS guards were in a state of near panic; most of their overheard talk predicted doom. April 20, 1945 was Adolf Hitler's fifty-sixth birthday. We listened to Dr. Goebbels' broadcast that evening. God, he said, has sent us this man and this crisis so we may testify to the miracle of redemption. The next day the crisis intensified; people were beginning to eat horse meat. Buildings were collapsing everywhere. Would this prison be next? I began to prepare for death, but there was no time. The end was approaching faster than anyone had thought possible. Once again, I tried to think back to the old days, the days of heartfelt joy and genuine comradeship. Nonetheless, these thoughts did not change reality. The Russians had broken through our lines and were now within the city limits. There was an important announcement on the radio: Hitler would stay in Berlin and defend it to the last. He would never leave. Never! I was surprised to hear this, but I must say that I was pleased. We would not die alone. At least, the leader of the nation would prefer death to dishonorable surrender. Also, I now felt that all our remaining armed forces would now rush to Berlin to defend the Fuehrer. This was not good for me: it would prolong the battle. I did not know then that there were no remaining army units. They had all been destroyed—mainly due to Hitler's stupidity and to superior enemy forces. (Oh, how we could use the Sixth Army, which had been sacrificed at Stalingrad!) You know, Hitler was right in one thing: Russia is a horrible country—the end of the world. And this abysmal world was now coming here. There were only a few German divisions left to halt them and, of course, the Hitler Youth. This was unknown then, but is certainly revealing of the nature of Nazism. Boys between the ages of fourteen and sixteen were being sacrificed to prolong Hitler's life a few days. Our world had gone completely mad. Goebbels was announcing that any street or houses displaying white flags would be detonated. We must fight to the death! I was hoping that I would be released to fight, but I realized that this was a forlorn wish. I was to die! Then, on April 24, an SS detachment approached my cell. I was ordered to dress and was led down a dimly lit corridor to a waiting truck. Several other prisoners were there, including Fabian. We were driven away. I knew in my heart that we would be shot, and I prepared mentally for death. I said a prayer. (Hitler meant nothing, but God did. We always turn to the true God in time of need.) The ride was horrible: explosions were occurring everywhere. Yet, it was also endless. I assumed that they would drive a short distance and shoot us, but apparently this was not their purpose. I later learned that the Gestapo was moving us out through the last remaining corridor west of the doomed capital. I was with important men even though I did not consider myself important: General Halder, Dr. Schacht, Schlabrendorff and Schuschnigg. The latter was the deposed Chancellor of Austria. They were all political prisoners with contacts overseas and were being kept alive for their contacts, which might prove useful to Himmler. Why was I included? It certainly was a mistake. I had no living friends in England—which is the way I wanted it. (I wish the whole island was an isle of the dead—except the whores. English whores are the best in the world!) Maybe, they thought I had contacts. I knew urinating on whores would be useful one day. Pleasure and business together! You see, the former chicken-farmer-turned-SS Chief was trying to take over the government, and Himmer needed international connections to arrange a peace behind Hitler's back. He failed in this—true believers make poor traitors—and was later sentenced to death, as was the vile, greedy Hermann Goering for the same treachery. The shabby nature of the Nazi regime began to show itself in the last days. They were all devouring each other with glee. Each thought only of himself—savage gods contemplating their own being. And I was no exception. As this endless ride continued, I briefly fell asleep and descended into a world of dreams.

I remember one dream in particular. I saw my grandmother, who had died twenty years before, walking on a barren road in the land of Egypt. I don't know how I knew this was Egypt; I just knew. A kindly woman whom I deeply loved; she was one of my few good childhood memories. She looked tired and beaten, and this disturbed me. The golden sun in the sky indicated that the heat must have been unbearable. When I woke, I was upset for some time. Why would I dream of her? And why was she in such a wretched condition? I could not understand. I quickly thought of other things. (Years later, however, I arrived at a different interpretation after reading Jung. The sun is an eternal symbol of wholeness, God, and redemption. And Egypt was the land of the gods and eternity. Now, I grasped the true meaning of the dream. Indeed, my grandmother's life on earth was hard, but she had finally attained eternal life with the true God in heaven.) Was this a message from God or only one from my collective unconscious? Was this, in short, the idle or purposeless working of my mind or a vision imprinted by God? In any case, I had no time to ponder the mystery. Mundane times leave room only for mundane considerations!

Finally, the truck stopped, and we were ordered out. I looked around at the dull landscape for what I thought would be my last vision of earth; we would certainly be shot now. My heart pounded. You know, death right now is much more frightening than death tomorrow. Yet, once again nothing happened! (Was I to die many deaths? If so, I cheated the executioner. I had already died nine hundred times. The death decreed by God was losing its terror. How great was Saint Paul: "To me, to live is Christ, and to die is gain." However he died, he died once. How great he was and how puny I am!) We apparently were just being given some time to stand up and walk. There were several other trucks, and it occurred to me that we were not going anywhere. We were being held captive on this motor caravan. There was no place to go; every important town and district was occupied by the enemy. I later learned that some trucks were filled with booty that the Gestapo had plundered. I felt so uprooted; I had nowhere to turn. (I almost wish there was a God: you could always depend on him.) My god was Adolf Hitler, and my hell had arrived. Satan was wrong: it is better to serve in heaven than to reign in hell. Yet, where was my devil? He was in a subterranean bunker directing nonexisting armies with his host of lackeys—above all, Martin Bormann. This wretched individual had accumulated massive power behind the scenes and was now the main authority in the state. He was using it to further his own ambition, which was none other than to be the next Fuehrer. Yes, my savage deity had lost his mind toward the end, and lesser gods were ready to replace him. But, he was still in control. (Ha, this was the man who would make us "lords of the earth.") I will never worship a secular deity again. Never!

On May 1, 1945, there was an announcement on the radio: Adolf Hitler was dead. The SS men had informed us that he had died fighting against the barbarian Russians. In spite of everything, I cried for Adolf Hitler. His death marked the passing of an age. Of course, he did not die fighting against Bolshevism. He committed suicide. He put a bullet through his right temple. He may also have swallowed poison—cyanide! In any case, his decision was the correct one: he died a soldier's death. And he died with freedom. If there is any true freedom, it lies in a decision on how and when to die. All life aims at the preservation of being. In deliberately choosing nonbeing, we negate all aspects of determination.

We should all die as Hitler did. Amid universal chaos and destruction—and by our own choice. Would it be better to die in a hospital at the mercy of uncaring and mercenary doctors? No, it would be better to point a blade at the doctor! (Hitler killed several of his personal physicians. How good of him! I wish I could have been there.) In any case, this business of being born free, struggling, and then dying of a vile disease has always repelled me. When I go, I hope it will be in battle while I'm pointing a gun at the world.

What is this world, anyhow? A vile and repulsive place. I never saw any value in it. And I could never understand why Christ would die to save this world. In this regard, I favored Buddhism over Christianity because Buddhist doctrine stressed the evils of existence. Actually, Christian beliefs also did—with less emphasis. God did destroy Sodom and Gomorrah. And in fact the whole age at the time of Noah. Christians talk constantly of the end of the world. What does this doctrine mean? It seems to imply that the world should be destroyed in its present form because it is selfish and base. Evil incarnate!

After Hitler's death, there was nothing left for the German people—just dishonorable surrender. In my life, there was only a void. The sun around which I orbited exploded! The caravan kept on traveling aimlessly, stopping at various intervals for no apparent reason. In a way, I hoped they would be kind and kill us; even death was better than this cruel existence. But, they didn't; they just kept on moving. During this interval, I exchanged a few words with Schlabrendorff. He told me how in 1931 he could have assassinated Hitler, before his rise to power. Fabian encountered him and his cronies in a tavern in Bavaria. Hitler was entirely unprotected and could easily have been killed. Fabian often thought, "If I had any idea of the degradation this man would cause, I would have done it without the least hesitation." And his thought was not without merit. I admired Fabian and respected him. I still do. The caravan, however, kept on moving and moving. When would the end come? How often could I prepare myself for death? After a while, you didn't care anymore! Finally, on May 4, the end came, but not as expected. An American unit near Niederdorf quickly surrounded and captured the entire caravan. The Gestapo had no time to kill us. We were free! Overjoyed, we gratefully entered American captivity. How ironical that I should be happy to be under American supervision. But, I was!

I was free, but had little will to live. I was interviewed by the Americans and was then assured that I would be released in due time. While I was being investigated, I was placed in a minimum detention area. Yet, there was not much difference from my former confinement! Normal rations, a modest cot, showers, and foreign newspapers. As usual, I kept to myself and read avidly. What a mess Hitler had made of things! Germany was entirely occupied and would be for decades. The people had nothing—not even a piece of bread. Our cities lay in ruins. And there was no fuel for the winter—tens of thousands would freeze to death. Germany no longer had any status as a great European power. Hitler had to be recorded as one of the greatest failures in history.

He, of course, did not live to pay for his crimes—others did. At Nuremberg, most high members of the Nazi government were sentenced to death, including Johl, Keitel, Kaltenbrunner, Frank, Frick, Rosenberg, Ribbentrop, Seyss-Inquart, Streicher, and Goering. Himmler and

Goebbels committed suicide before these events. I still believe that the trials at Nuremberg were only what might be called victors' justice. Most despicable was the conduct of the Russian and the American jurists. America's leader used the atomic bomb on two cities in Japan, causing untold civilian destruction. And Stalin murdered more than thirty million people. Who the hell gave these two nations the right to judge us? The force of arms, of course—and only that. But, at other times, I have felt differently. The crimes of the men at Nuremberg were unconscionable. For example, Goering deserved to die for building the first concentration camps. Keitel and Johl deserved death for being Hitler's willing accomplices in the military. And Kaltenbrunner merited the highest penalty for his substantial part in the terror. Hitler could never had committed these crimes alone; they were all part of the conspiracy against mankind.

When I was young, cultural relativism was popular in England. One man's morals were as good as his neighbor's, and every culture's moral ideas were as good as those of any of the rest. What a mistake! No man of good common sense could believe this in 1945. The death camps and the systematic killing of millions had put an end to that. It seemed obvious that there must be an absolute standard, a standard by which we could judge all moral conduct. And that standard, perhaps, did derive from God. Why else should man, a creature of flesh and blood, care about his fellow man? Certainly, not on the basis of materialism! If morals are absolute, they indirectly point to a world beyond the natural order, that is, beyond the natural passions and the desire for self-preservation. And there is nothing natural about moral judgements since they are often quite contrary to private self-interest. Kant once said that two things made him believe in God: the starry heavens above and the moral consciousness within. And he could have been right.

In any case, I was discharged the following month and for a time wandered aimlessly. Nowhere to go, nothing to do. And no friends. Nothing had changed. How I lived after my subsequent immigration to England and later to America is too boring and inconsequential to be recapitulated here. Anyway, some secrets must be buried with me! I reside today in New York City, a city of smut and selfishness. In my dotage, I live in a world of ideas with few friends. I enjoy listening to Bob Grant on the radio. I enjoy the New York Mets and more. But, as the saying goes, when life gives, it does so only to take. I now face a cancer diagnosis and anticipate my speedy demise. I could not be more detached from life than I am now.

The doctors recommended surgery and cancer medication. All designed, no doubt, to make Doctors Dosik, Marcus, and Gingrus rich. But, I had a better solution to my problem. You know, the best feeling on earth is having a Beretta with eight bullets in it and running into a doctor ready to use his knife. Now, a strange situation exists: the patient is alive and the doctors are quite dead. Yes, dead! "Doctor Dosik, will you take a check or shall it be cash? Ha, you bastard! That bullet in your throat is your just payment. When you started this game of slow torture, you didn't know that I treasure a painting of Adolf Hitler. Yes, Dosik! Adolf Hitler!" I raised my right arm. "Heil Hitler!"

"And Doctor Marcus—a woman! I like women doctors—I like them dead as that bullet in your head reveals. How insensitive you were to my suffering! Now, I am insensitive when I urinate on your stinking corpse. A kidney specialist! I'll cut out your dead kidney and feed it to a bulldog! Ha, you hole. You hole!" I raised my right arm again. "Heil Hitler!"

"And Doctor Gingrus. I must not forget you! You dog! Did you think running would save you? I don't think so—not with several bullets in your back. I heard that you were going to Africa this summer—ha, I'll ship your corpse to Angola! Great trip!" I raised my right arm in a final Nazi salute. "Heil Hitler, Heil Hitler, Heil Hitler!"

The two major passions of my life were Jesus Christ and Adolf Hitler. I talked much of Christ, but did not live the will of Christ. As the saying goes, "Words without thoughts never to heaven go." I am now a prisoner of Adolf Hitler and his master, the "Prince of the Power of the Air," who, no doubt, brought him down to destruction.

What is this memoir? Perhaps, it is a cry, an isolated moan of desperation, or the yearning of one who is forgotten. Yet, it is more than that. It is, also, a gesture of acquiescence, a belated recognition of the fact that what has happened has happened! We can neither change nor escape the past. No doubt, we can recall, interpret, and debate. But, the past is oblivious to all this: it simply endures. So here I acknowledge the finality of my expired days and the events they envelop. I accept that this happened. It really happened!

Today, I think only of essences, lost essences. What is life but a continual search for lost essences. Lost days, lost thoughts, lost loves. Love of man, I lost long ago. Love of self, I lose now—with a pistol shot!

NOTES AND BIBLIOGRAPHY

1. Alfred Adler. A psychologist and founder of a major psychotherapy known as Individual Psychology. He placed great emphasis on the role of ideas and purposive human behavior.

2. Anaximander. A pre-Socratic philosopher who put forward one of the first ideas of evolution. He also contributed to metaphysics and cosmology.

3. Aristotle. An ancient Greek philosopher who is best known for his contributions to logic, ethics, and metaphysics. With Plato, he embodies the classic period of Greek philosophy.

4. Attila. He led the Huns to invade Gaul, where the Romans stopped him near Paris in the year 451 A.D. He was known as the "Scourge of God."

5. Ludwig van Beethoven. He was known best for his greatest symphony, which he called the *Eroica*. His music reflected the striving and changing moods of life and society in a dramatic fashion.

6. Otto von Bismarck. A great Prussian Chancellor who achieved the unification of Germany by force in 1871. He was greatly admired by Adolf Hitler and generations of German youth. Unlike Hitler, he died having achieved great success and recognition as the founder of the Reich.

7. Martin Bormann. One of Hitler's closest aides from 1941 until 1945. He was named Party Minister in Hitler's Last Will and Testament. He died trying to escape Berlin after Hitler's death.

8. Walter Von Brauchitsch. Commander-in-Chief of the German Army until 1941.

9. Martin Buber. A philosopher who is best known for his book, *I and Thou*. He was mainly concerned with the manner in which one relates to the world of material things, to other men, and to God. "I-Thou" is the proper method of relating or accepting other beings in all their wholeness. "I-It" is improper being a mode of exploitation or rejection of another beings.

10. Edmund Burke. A British statesman who defended the American Revolution in 1776 as an attempt to preserve traditional rights and liberties. He is also known for his philosophical writings.

11. Caesar Augustus. The first and greatest emperor of ancient Rome after his famous uncle was assassinated. He reigned from 27 B.C. to 14 A.D.

12. Houston Stewart Chamberlain. An English racist writer who later immigrated to Germany. His famous publication was *The Foundations of the Nineteenth Century*. His main idea was that race is the key to history. He also was among the first to see a great career for Hitler—as early as 1923.

13. Giorgio de Chirico. An Italian painter best known for his metaphysical paintings. One of his most famous works, *The Great Metaphysician*, presents his attempt to reveal the hidden meaning behind the surface of objects. In viewing his paintings, one sees the world without the filter of memory.

14. Charles Darwin. He formulated the first modern theory of evolution in 1859. Although derived from early Greek sources, his was a scientific theory supported by empirical evidence. His theory has since been reformulated to fit the findings of genetics and other technical fields.

15. John Dewey. He was an American philosopher of education. He emphasized the role of experience and instrumentalism in the educational process.

16. Dietrich Eckart. He is known as the spiritual founder of the National Socialist Workers Party. He was also a poet and a playwright.

17. Hermann Esser. One of Hitler's followers in the early days of the struggle in Munich.

18. Albert Einstein. He formulated the General and Special Theories of Relativity in physics. Much of his overall theory, however, has since been revised and overturned by other physicists. He signed a letter to President Franklin D. Roosevelt urging the development of the atomic bomb. Years before, he left Germany to advance his studies at Princeton University.

19. Johann Gottlieb Fichte. A German philosopher best known for his work, *The Vocation of Man*. He advocated a primacy of a system of posits: we posit the Ego as well as the non-Ego, which evolved into many advanced concepts in his broad metaphysical system.

20. James Franck. A professor of physics who was forced to retire after Hitler's rise to power.

21. Hans Frank. He was appointed Governor General of Poland in 1939 by Hitler. He was responsible for the deaths of hundreds of thousands of Poles during the Nazi occupation. He was sentenced to death at Nuremberg and executed in 1946.

22. Roland Freisler. The President and Chief Justice of the People's Court in Nazi Germany. He handed down numerous death sentences before he was killed during an American bombing of Berlin on February 3, 1945. He is today buried in an unmarked grave.

23. Sigmund Freud. A medical psychologist who invented the theory of psychoanalysis. He emphasized the importance of the unconscious mind and the hidden meaning behind ordinary dreams. His most important publication was, *The Interpretation of Dreams*, which was published in 1899. He is, also, known for his theory of the death instinct in man and many other significant concepts.

24. Wilhelm Frick. He was the Minister of the Interior under Hitler. He was sentenced to death and hanged at Nuremberg in 1946.

25. Count Joseph Arthur de Gobineau. A French racist writer who believed that race was the key concept in understanding history. His most significant work was *The Essay on the Inequality of the Human Races*, which was published in 1855.

26. Dr. Joseph Goebbels. He was the Minister for Propaganda and Popular Enlightenment under Hitler. He committed suicide on May 1, 1945.

27. Johann Wolfgang Goethe. A German poet and philosopher. He also mastered the fields of botany, geology, and optics and is regarded as one of the great, universal minds in history. His great work was *Faust,* which has had wide influence on the later history of literature.

28. Hermann Goering. He was Reichsmarshal and Chief of the Luftwaffe. He was, also, responsible for building the first concentration camps in 1933 and was sentenced to death at Nuremberg for crimes against humanity in 1946. However, he committed suicide before the sentence could be carried out.

29. Bob Grant. He was a conservative talk show host on New York radio in 1970.

30. Fritz Haber. A German chemist who was forced to leave his university post after Hitler's rise to power.

31. Fritz Halder. The Army Chief of Staff. He was fired by Hitler in 1942 and later sent to a concentration camp. He was freed by American units in May 1945.

32. Hannibal. A great Carthaginian general who invaded ancient Rome in 217 B.C. He was later defeated at Zama by the Roman general, Scipio.

33. Georg Wilhelm Friedrich Hegel. A German philosopher who emphasized the importance of a dialectic of reason in history. His best known work , *The Phenomenology of Mind,* was published in 1807.

34. Martin Heidegger. A German philosopher known for his study of ontology, the philosophy of being. His greatest work , *Being and Time,* was published in 1927. He was a Nazi and praised Hitler during his years at the University of Freiburg.

35. Heraclitus. An ancient Greek philosopher who had a profound influence on all subsequent thought. His great ideas include that of the *logos,* the tension of opposites and the concept of eternal flux.

36. Rudolf Hess. He was Deputy Fuehrer and second in line to succeed Hitler until 1941. He voluntarily flew to England that year in the mistaken belief that he could arrange a peace settlement. He was later sentenced to life imprisonment at Nuremberg for his involvement in the Nazi regime. He died in prison.

37. Reinhard Heydrich. Head of the SS Security Service or SD. He was assassinated in 1942.

38. Heinrich Himmler. The SS Fuehrer of the Third Reich. He was responsible for the deaths of millions in the extermination camps. He committed suicide in May 1945 in order to avoid capture.

39. Paul von Hindenburg. The President of the Weimar Republic until his death in 1934.

40. Adolf Hitler. The Fuehrer and absolute dictator of Nazi Germany from 1933 until his death in 1945. He was the most important historical figure of his time. He had a firm belief that he was the savior of the German nation. He was born in Linz, Austria, on

April 20, 1889. His early life was one of great difficulties: he hated his father who died in 1903 and lost his beloved mother to cancer in 1908. From then until 1913, he lived the life of a vagabond. In 1914, he enlisted in the German army and served with distinction until he was wounded in a British gas attack in 1918. In the hospital, he learned of Germany's surrender on November 11, 1918. He never could accept this defeat. He reasoned that the Fatherland had been stabbed in the back by Jews and traitorous democrats. And he vowed revenge. He joined a small group of men—later to be called the Nazi party. He possessed great powers of oratory and intellect and slowly led this movement to absolute power in Germany. Once in control, he allowed no freedom: every aspect of the nation was controlled by him. The Jews were marked out for extermination, and Hitler's foreign policy was most aggressive. In 1939, he attacked Poland, which resulted in a general war. He later destroyed France, but his attack on Russia backfired and resulted in massive German loses. After America entered the war, Germany's fate was sealed. By 1945, foreign armies occupied almost all of the nation. Hitler committed suicide on April 30, 1945.

41. David Hume. A Scottish philosopher who is best known for his book *Dialogues Concerning Natural Religion,* in which he cast doubt on the traditional argument for design in nature by God. He died in 1776.

42. Alfred Jodl. A German general and close advisor to Adolf Hitler. At Nuremberg, he was sentenced to death and hanged in 1946.

43. Carl Jung. A Swiss psychologist and philosopher. He believed that archetypal patterns or symbols common to all mankind are revealed in dreams and mythology. He died in 1961.

44. Ernst Kaltenbrunner. He was a SS Obergruppenfuehrer. At Nuremberg, he was sentenced to death and hanged in 1946.

45. Immanuel Kant. He was a German philosopher who greatly influenced the history of that field. He is best known for the publication of his three critiques: *A Critique of Pure Reason, A Critique of Practical Reason, and A Critique of Judgment.* He is also known for other important works on religion, ethics, and theology. He was truly one of the most monumental minds in history.

46. General Korten. A general and military advisor to Hitler who died of wounds received in the assassination attempt on the Fuehrer's life on July 20, 1944.

47. August Kubizek. Adolf Hitler's only boyhood friend before 1909.

48. Gottfried Wilhelm Leibniz. A great German metaphysician and rationalist philosopher. He is best known for his work *Monadology,* which was published in 1714.

49. Martin Luther. The founder of the Lutheran Church and the most important spiritual leader during the Protestant Reformation. He also greatly influenced the history of Germany.

50. Karl Marx. A political philosopher who despised the capitalist system and advocated a form of scientific socialism. Hitler hated Marx and regarded his ideas as Jewish in origin. Marx is best known for his work *Capital,* which was published in 1886.

51. Gregor Mendel. An Austrian abbot who greatly influenced the development of genetics.

52. Dr. Theodor Morell. Adolf Hitler's personal physician.

53. Napoleon I. Emperor of the French. He established a great European empire by 1812. After his defeat, he was exiled to St. Helena, where he died in 1821. Hitler admired Napoleon and visited his tomb in Paris in 1940.

54. Friedrich Nietzsche. A German philosopher and poet. He often extolled the irrational in human nature but still advocated the doctrine of the overman, a man who was qualitatively superior to ordinary humans. Hitler admired Nietzsche and visited his museum in Weimar, where the philosopher had died in 1900. Nietzsche's most important book, *Thus Spoke Zarathustra,* was published in 1891.

55. Friedrich Paulus. A Field Marshal and commander of the ill-fated Sixth Army at Stalingrad. He ordered a general surrender there on February 2, 1943. Hitler had ordered him to hold on and fight to the last man and the last round. Paulus did not. He went into captivity and was released after the war. Hitler despised Paulus and regarded him as a coward and a defeatist.

56. Plato. An ancient Greek thinker who is clearly the world's most influential philosopher. His greatest work was *The Republic,* in which he presents his ideas on the ideal state. He is also known for his famous dialogues featuring Socrates. He died in 348 B.C.

57. Vidkun Quisling. The Norwegian traitor who betrayed his country to help Nazi Germany in 1940. After the war, Quisling was sentenced to death and executed in 1945.

58. Rasputin. A self-appointed holy man who had great influence over Tsar Nicholas II and his wife during World War I. He was assassinated in 1916.

59. Joachim von Ribbentrop. A German Foreign Minister under Hitler. He was sentenced to death at Nuremberg and executed in 1946.

60. Ernst Roehm. The leader of the SA who was killed on June 30, 1934.

61. Erwin Rommel. A German Field Marshal who achieved great victories in North Africa in 1940-41. He was forced by Hitler to kill himself in 1944.

62. Franklin D. Roosevelt. An American President who served in that capacity between 1933 and 1945.

63. Alfred Rosenberg. A German racist writer and Nazi official who was appointed by Hitler to organize a mass terror in Russia. At Nuremberg, he was sentenced to death and hanged in 1946.

64. Saint Paul. Christianity's greatest missionary and, perhaps, its greatest theologian.

65. Baldur von Schirach. The first leader of the Hitler Youth.

66. Fabian von Schlabrendorff. One of the most important conspirators against Hitler. He was sentenced to death by the People's Court but later freed by American units in the South Tyrol at Niederdorf.

67. Arthur Schopenhauer. A great German metaphysician who believed that pure will, not reason, is at the ground of reality. He was one of the first thinkers to describe the irrational mature of man. He is best known for his work *The World As Will and Representation,* which was published in 1818.

68. Kurt von Schuschnigg. The Chancellor of Austria who was jailed after the Nazis occupied that country in 1938. He also spent some time in a concentration camp before he was freed by American units at Niederdorf on May 4, 1945.

69. William Shakespeare. A great master of English drama and poetry.

70. Albert Speer. Hitler's personal architect and head of war production. He was sentenced to twenty years in prison at Nuremberg.

71. Benedict de Spinoza. A great Jewish philosopher and metaphysician. His best known work, *The Ethics,* was published after his early death in 1677.

72. Joseph Stalin. Dictator of the Soviet Union from 1924 to 1953.

73. Count Von Stauffenberg. The main conspirator in a plot against Hitler on July 20, 1944. He placed a bomb near the dictator's legs. Count Stauffenberg was killed the next day by Nazi loyalists.

74. Gregor Strasser. A Nazi leader during the early phase of the movement. He was often associated with socialist ideas that Hitler later abandoned. He was killed on Goering's orders on June 30, 1934.

75. Julius Streicher. The Nazi chief in Franconia. He was executed in 1946.

76. Thales. The first great ancient Greek philosopher in the city-state of Miletus. He had many ideas, including the belief that water is the first principle of all things.

77. Ernst Thaelmann. A communist leader in Germany during the Weimar Republic. His political party was later destroyed by Hitler.

78. Publius Quintilius Varus. A commander of the ill-fated Roman army that was destroyed by Arminius in 9 A.D

79. Franz von Papen. The Vice-Chancellor of the in the early Hitler government in 1933-1934.

80. Professor Warburg. A great chemist who was forced to leave his university after Hitler's rise to power.

81. Christian Weber. One of Hitler's early followers during his Munich period. He was, also, a noted horse dealer.

82. Dr. Weissmann. A court-appointed defense lawyer who represented the conspirators during their trial before the People's Court in 1944.

83. Alfred North Whitehead. A great British philosopher and metaphysician. He was, also, an important figure in physics and mathematics. He is known for his work *Process and Reality: An Essay in Cosmology,* which was published in 1929.

84. Wilhelm II. The Kaiser who ruled Germany during World War I. He was forced into exile in 1918. Hitler despised him and made sure that there was no mention in the press of his death in 1941.

85. Ludwig Wittgenstein. An Austrian philosopher who is best known for his book, *Philosophical Investigations,* which was published in 1953.

BIBLIOGRAPHY

Bullock, Alan, *Hitler: a Study in Tryanny*, Harper Perennial, New York, 1991.

Fest, Joachim, *Hitler*, Harcourt, Brace and Jovanovich Publishers, New York, 1973.

Hart, Liddell, B.H., *History of the Second World War*, G.P. Putnam's Sons, New York, 1970.

Kershaw, Ian, *Hitler, 1936-45: Nemesis*, W.W. Norton & Company, New York and London, 2000.

Langer, Walter C., *A Psychological Analysis of Adolf Hitler: His Life and Legend*, Office of Strategic Services Report, National Archives, 1943.

Shirer, William L., *The Rise and Fall of the Third Reich: A History of Nazi Germany*, Simon and Schuster, New York, 1960.

Speer, Albert, *Inside the Third Reich*, Macmillian, New York, 1970.

Toland, John, *Adolf Hitler*, Doubleday Anchor Books, New York, 1976.

Trevor-Roper, Hugh, *The Last Days of Hitler*, Sixth Edition, University of Chicago Press, Chicago, 1987.

Waite, Robert, G.L., *The Psychopathic God: Adolf Hitler*, Da Capo Press, New York, 1993.